Indigenous Manpower In the Private Sector Of the Arabian Peninsula

A Guide to Effective Achievement

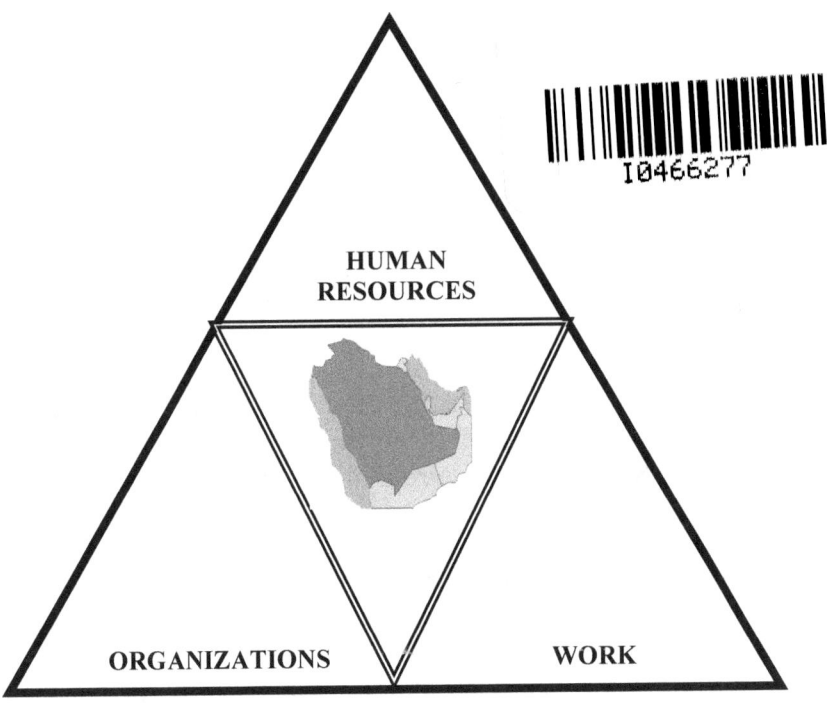

Samir S. Ghazal

Second Edition

Mr. Samir S. Ghazal is ex Human Resources Manager at the Saudi Aramco Mobil Refinery Company Ltd. (SAMREF) Yanbu, Saudi Arabia. He retired from employment mid-2010.

Mr. Ghazal has a Master Degree in Human Resources Management from the USA and over thirty five years of working experience in Saudi Arabia.

He is a member of many associations both locally and globally. He is currently having his own YouTube channel under his name tackling various HR issues and management subjects.

بسم الله الرحمن الرحيم

In the Name of Allah, the Most Beneficent, the Most Merciful

"By Al- Asr (the time) ❊ Verily! Man is in loss ❊ Except those who believe and do righteous deeds and recommend one another to truth and recommend one another to patience ❊".

Surah Al-Asr
The Holy Qur'an

"The state's concern for national manpower is not a mere slogan. It is a clearly stated objective we are working hard to achieve. Many quarters are deeply engaged in studies and plans aimed at absorbing nationals in the economic sector in accordance with the requirements of the development process and the need for productivity."

The Custodian of The Two Holy Mosques
King Fahad ibn Abdulaziz
Saudi Gazette, January 2, 1997

DEDICATION

I dedicate this book (second edition) to:

To all genuinely interested parties and individuals in the localization of workforce.

CONTENTS

Preface	xi
Acknowledgment	xiii

PART I The Conventional Relationship

1 The Private Sector	11
2 Manpower	18
3 Employment	25

PART II The Influencing Factors

4 Variables	32
5 Environment	37
6 Values	42

PART III The Practical Look

7 Expatriates	51
8 Requirements	59
9 Investment	66

CONTENTS

PART IV The Replacement Program

10	Evaluate the Business	77
11	Establish the Plan	83
12	Execute the Plan	91

Part V *The Kingdom Of Saudi Arabia*

13	Development in Focus	100
14	Saudization in Practice	108
15	Challenges for the Future	122

Bibliography   130

Appendixes   134

Index   136

PREFACE

First edition (1997)

During the past thirty years or so, the Arabian Peninsula has undergone rapid and major developments including the development of its human resources. However, due to the magnitude of development, its pace and the advanced technology associated with such development, the region's human resources were unable at the time, to cope with the newly created demand. The fact that the indigenous work force was scarce made the situation more challenging. This situation has compelled the region to rely on an expatriate workforce to perform the work, educate and train the nationals.

With the increasing supply of the indigenous work force, emphasis on replacing the expatriates became imperative. This is now increasingly evident in the business organizations (private sector) as they remain to be the major employers of expatriates in the region.

Many organizations realize that having more of an indigenous work force is inevitable. They also realize that it is the right thing to do. It is the way to genuine growth and development of the region.

However, replacing the workforce from mainly expatriates to mostly indigenous demands a major change in the organization. This is not simply a replacement exercise. Apart from changing faces at the workplace and figures in the payroll, changing the work force is, in essence, a transformation of the organizational culture and ways of doing business.

The emphasis on an indigenous workforce comes at a time when globalization is at our doorsteps and businesses are already experiencing other challenges due to high competition.

The mergers and acquisitions, reengineering, out-sourcing, downsizing (rightsizing), and recent pandemic (Corona-covid 19) are some of these challenges.

This book is designed to guide those who are willing to face this challenge and respond to the changing world of human resources.

This book consists of five parts with three chapters each. The first part deals with definitions, concepts and the relationship between organizations, human resources, and work. The second part focuses on factors that influence having an effective manpower. The third part gives an insight of the expatriates working in the Peninsula [mainly the Gulf Cooperation Council (GCC) countries]. Requirements of individuals (employees), organizations (employers) and that of work along with investment in national manpower are also being discussed in this part. The fourth part proposes a workable replacement program of expatriates.

Finally, the fifth part summarizes related development in the Kingdom of Saudi Arabia with a highlight to the Saudization process that is taking place in three major industries. Chapter fifteen ends the book by outlining thought provoking future changes and challenges in the region. The first edition was printed by Kegan Paul International, London, UK.

Second edition (2021)

In this second edition, I hardly made any modifications, changes, or updates. I wanted the original thoughts, people I came in contact, business conditions, employment status, and figures to be remembered as it was back in 1997 when I first wrote the book. This is in addition to the fact that the essence and principles of the book is still valid after more than 24 years of its first publication. This edition is printed by Lulu.com.

ACKNOWLEDGMENTS

My deepest appreciation and gratitude are extended to my family for their endless support and patience. My thanks to my colleagues at work who also supported me during this endeavor especially to Tzehaie Abraha, Aboud A. Baqais, Sami H. Ghulam, Saeed M. Al-Ghamdi and last, but certainly not least, Shahzad Akhtar. I am also grateful to Mr. Adel A. Fadel, Mr. Ali S. KhairAlla from Saudi Aramco and to Mr. Marwan Y. Kutbi from ABV. Also, I should not forget Ahmad R. Al-Jayyousi of almajal *ServiceMASTER*.

I also wish to thank the Institute for International Research (IIR), Dr. Ahmed Fetyani, Training and Development Manager at National Commercial Bank (NCB) and Dr. Muhammad A. Al-Buraey at King Fahad University of Petroleum and Minerals (KFUPM).

Part I

THE CONVENTIONAL RELATIONSHIP

PRIVATE SECTOR

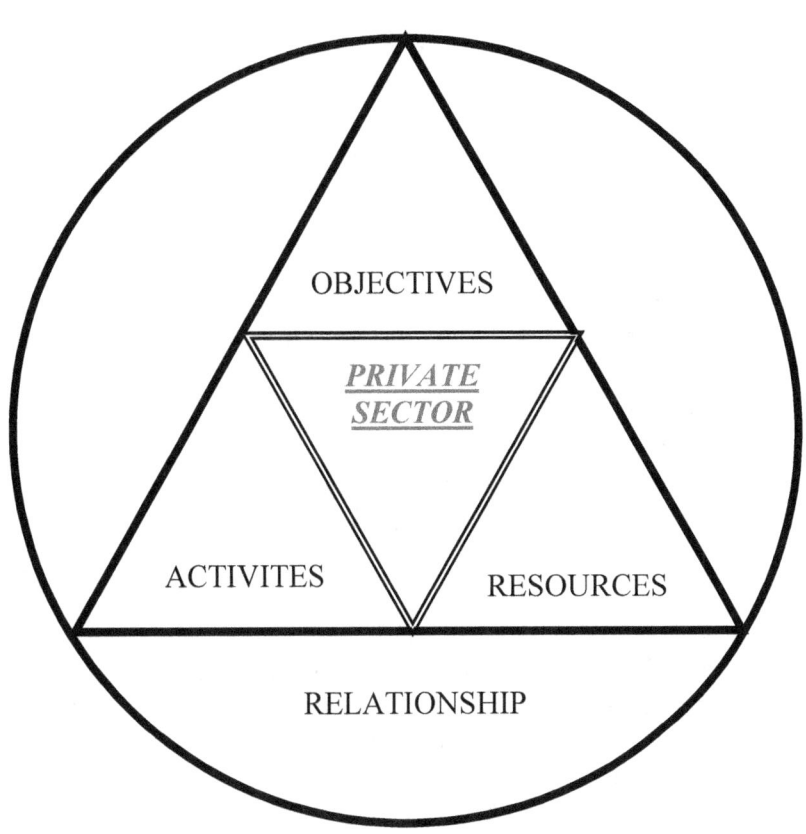

CHAPTER 1

The Private Sector

The intent of this chapter is to give the reader a comprehensive and concise view of the private sector. Since the private sector is one of the formal organizations, the author finds it appropriate to begin by addressing the types and the core purposes of these organizations. **Formal organizations** in the Arabian Peninsula that are known to employ a large work force can be divided into four different types:

1- **Military:** These are government organizations mainly concerned with the safety, security, and stability of the nation.

2- **Public:** These are also government organizations except they deal with the civil affairs; and therefore, their tasks are to provide products and services to the people. In the Peninsula, some of these services are provided for free such as education and medical care. Other services are obtained for a subsidized cost as in the case of utilities.

3- **Semiprivate:** These types of organizations are mainly joint ventures between the government and other business entities. They may either be local or foreign entities. Most of these ventures offer some stocks or shares to the public. Such ventures can be clearly noted in the oil, gas and petrochemical industries.

4- **Private:** These organizations are either profit or nonprofit driven. They are privately owned and under a proprietorship, partnership, stockholders' ownership, or a combination of the latter two. In the Arabian Peninsula, due to the need of technology and know-how, a great number of these organizations are also joint ventures with other international business organizations from the industrialized nations.

In this book, the focus is on the private and **profit oriented** organizations only. They are called **the private sector.** To understand the private sector somewhat better, let us explore their common objectives, activities and resources.

OBJECTIVES

The prime **objectives** of the private sector can be summed up and best described as:

1- **Investment security:** One of the pivotal concerns of the private sector is to ensure that their investments are secure. This security becomes obvious when the political environment encourages such investments and funds can be freely transferred to and from the country. The Arabian Peninsula is known to be one of the best locations in
the world that provides such security to business organizations. It is also known to be a very safe place to live in.

2- **Profitability:** At the time of making the feasibility study and prior to investing, the private sector will proceed with a project only if it makes money and has a good rate of return; otherwise, it becomes a dead issue. Profitability is the major motive of the private sector for producing products and or services to the marketplace.

3- **Growth:** As the business is making money, the private sector is exploring ways and means of maximizing their profits. Growth is a result of expansion. It is the answer to generating more profit, especially on a long-term basis. Reducing costs and improving productivity do not, in themselves, provide real growth. However, they could provide incentive for growth.

4- **Reliability:** In order for the private sector to maintain its businesses, one of their objectives is to be reliable in their dealings with their customers, suppliers, employees and the community in general.

5- **Quality:** Offering good quality products and services is a key objective of any business organization. In addition to price, this is where competition among businesses takes place.

ACTIVITIES

After defining the common objectives of the private sector, let us quickly analyze the **business activities** that are being pursued in the Arabian Peninsula. These activities can be divided into five main categories:

1- **Industrial:** Since the early seventies, industrial cities and parks throughout the Peninsula were made available for private investors. As a result, thousands of factories and plants were erected for the purpose of producing desired goods. Due to the scarcity of the national work force as opposed to the availability of capital resources, the private sector has concentrated on technology that minimizes the employment of human resources. The lines of productions of those industries are mostly:

    A- Food, dairy products and drinks
    B- Plastic goods
    C- Office / home furniture and carpets
    D- Air conditioners
    E- Paint
    F- Building materials, tiles and bricks
    G- Safety shoes
    H- Industrial pipes and cables

2- **Operations and maintenance:** As a result of the many turnkey projects, demand for new businesses were created to handle the operations and maintenance activities of these projects once they are handed over. Power plants, desalinization plants and hospitals are some of the organizations that use the services of the private sector in the filed of operations and maintenance.

3- **Building and contracting:** The most common agreement adapted by these organizations is the 'turnkey' method. Here is where the contractor is responsible for the whole project (from A to Z) including its construction, equipment, and furniture.

4- **Agricultural:** The government also plays a major role in inviting investors to develop the vast dry lands and turn them into fertile soil. As a result, many local crops became available especially wheat, vegetables, fruits and flowers.

5- **Trading and services:** Like agriculture, trading is not a new line of business in the Arabian Peninsula. Nevertheless, it has expanded in recent years. This is where you will find international companies and manufacturers being represented in forms of agencies like automotive, heavy equipment and PC dealers. Services on the other hand, is becoming a new industry in itself and growing rapidly. The major fields of services are:

A- Banking
B- Education
C- Medical, Dental and Health care
D- Transportation and Shipping
E- Janitorial and Cleaning services
F- Tourism and Hotels
G- Catering
H- Real estate

RESOURCES

It is evident that the private sector needs resources to be able to do business and achieve desired objectives. Without resources, the business cannot be formed. The availability and low cost of resources in any given location is its business attraction.

Resources are summarized as follows:

1- **Natural:** The natural resources are those apparent to all of us and can be found on the planet earth. These are mountains, oceans, rivers, sand, land, trees, air, sun and the like. They also refer to the minerals, coal, crude oil and gases that are hidden in the inner earth.

The Arabian Peninsula is blessed with the largest reserve of crude oil in the world. Natural gas and minerals are also available. Sunlight and Seawater are abundant.

2- Produced: The produced resources are, in essence, processed natural resources used as raw materials for producing other products and services. The plastic industry is an example of a user of produced resources. The infrastructure that a country build can also be part of the produced resources.

3- Capital: The capital resources are often referred to as produced resources. However, for the purpose of this book, the capital resources are defined as the ability of an individual, an organization or a country to finance a project or an event. It is the money that can be made available as and when needed. Since the big hike of oil prices in 1973, the Peninsula's capital resources became so huge that a surplus budget ran for quite some years.

4- Technology and information: These resources are relatively new. After the industrial revolution (mechanization) of the 1750s, automation in the 1930s and the invention of computers in the 1940s, technology is becoming a very important resource. It is now playing a major role in shaping our lives and the lives of organizations. Technology has not only made things easier and faster, but processes information like never before. The information that all businesses need in order to survive in the ever-changing world is becoming at their disposal.

5- Human: The most important resource on earth is human resources. It is for them, that all other resources were made available in this universe.

The human resources are the link between the organizations and work. Organizations are always after the resources, which can only be found in the human species. These resources and more are the subject of the next chapter.

SUMMARY

In chapter one, types of formal organizations in the Arabian Peninsula were introduced. The military, public, semiprivate and the private organizations are the four main types of formal organizations. The private organizations are either profit or non-profit driven. The private and profit oriented organizations are called the 'private sector'.

In order for the private sector to run their businesses in a business-like manner, objectives must be set, activities are to be defined and resources should be attainable. The following table illustrates the most common objectives, activities and resources related to the world of private sector in the Peninsula.

OBJECTIVES	ACTIVITIES	RESOURCES
Investment security	Industrial	Natural
Profitability	Operations & Maintenance	Produced
Growth	Building & Contracting	Capital
Reliability	Agricultural	Technology & Information
Quality	Trading & Services	Human

MANPOWER

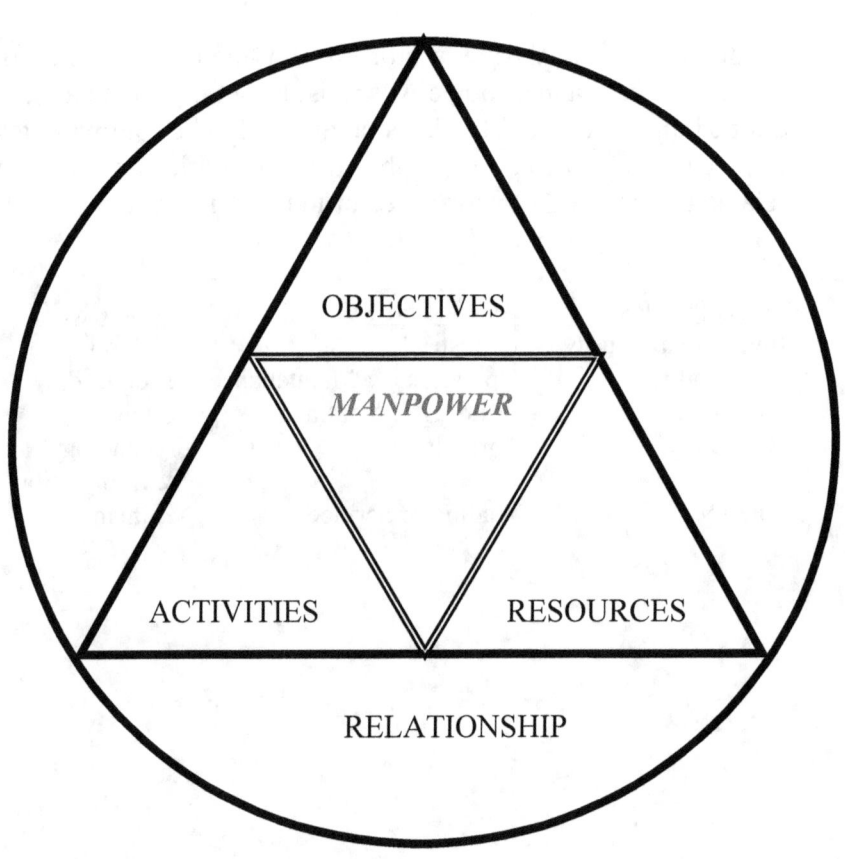

CHAPTER 2

Manpower

We have concluded the previous chapter by indicating that the human resource is one of the resources that all organizations must have. This chapter will focus on the *manpower* that is a segment of the human resources. However, before we proceed and to give additional clarification, let us make a distinction between manpower, work force and human resources.

When the word **human resources** are mentioned, it refers to the following types of people including those who are physically or mentally disabled:

1- **Elderly:** Males and females who are retired from work or cannot work due to old age. They are basically above 60 years of age.

2- **Juveniles:** Males and females who are fairly too young to work. They are children, below 16 years of age and are not fully-grown.

It is worth mentioning that unlike many developing countries, elderly and juveniles in the Arabian Peninsula are not employed.

3- **Women:** Females who are between the ages of 16 and 60. These are the most productive years of the humankind.

4- **Men:** Males who are also between the ages of 16 and 60. Again this is the working age where the men are young, strong and active.

The word *workforce,* however, refers to those males and females who are willing, able, and available to work. In this book, the focus will be on **the male** workforce. It is called *the manpower.*

It should be noted however, that this is not to underestimate the important role of the female work force, in any way, shape or form. The services of female doctors, teachers, nurses, computer operators and the like are always needed. The female contribution to the development of the nation is as valuable as that of the male work force. It is the author's conscious decision to concentrate on the male work force at this point of time. Nevertheless, in this book, there will be references, statistics, principles as well as theories that apply to the females as well.

Reverting to the subject and to have an appreciation of the indigenous manpower or the male work force of the Arabian Peninsula, their objectives, activities, and resources need to be addressed.

OBJECTIVES

The common objectives of the national male work force are listed in order of maturity and needs. These **objectives** that the subject nationals try to achieve during their lifetime are as follows:

1- **Independence:** It is of human nature that as one approaches the age of adolescence he begins to think of how and when he can become independent. Knowing that a steady income is the path to independence, nationals are motivated to complete their education and hence start their working life.

2- **Raising a family:** Once a job has been secured, the second objective is to get married. Therefore, you will find that during the first years of employment, most of the young workforce is preparing themselves for this big event. Needless to say, that parents and relatives play a major role in making this marriage possible. In the Peninsula, even though arranged marriages and marrying kin are common, still marriages can be very costly. For that, close relatives often contribute either in cash or in kind.

3- **Owning properties:** Buying a car is very much a necessity now days. Once that is accomplished, to ensure that the individual and his family have a place to live in that they can call their own become the second objective. This is provided that he does not already own a house (it is possible that one can inherit such property in the Peninsula especially if he comes from a well-to-do family). After that and depending on where he lives and how close to the coast, buying a boat is another property some would also like to have, as nationals tend to enjoy the sea. For cost and companion purposes, it is common to share the ownership of a boat with others. On the other hand, as the size of the family increases, many nationals tend to purchase bigger cars in order to accommodate all members. This action will eventually lead to owning two cars. The big car is for the family while a smaller one is for daily use.

4- **Improving living standards:** This usually comes to surface when the proceeding objectives have been accomplished. At this stage of one's life, ways and means of improving income and status in the society become the main objectives. Unfortunately, some nationals go beyond their means and needs to buy things or recruit housemaids just because it is a "status" to have one.

5- **Leaving a legacy:** Toward the peak of man's life, say in his forties, he starts thinking of the accomplishments he has made thus far. What he is going to leave for his beloved ones after his death becomes a concern. In the Arabian Peninsula, leaving a legacy, is not limited to materialism. Leaving a perpetual remembrance in the form of good deed, such as building a mosque is also common.

ACTIVITIES

Having discussed the individuals' objectives, let us now explore what are their day-to-day **activities**? Where most do, they go and what do they do? Our attempt to answer these questions is as follows:

1- **Work:** The average time spent at work is 8 hours daily. Most nationals, due to overwhelming family and/or social commitments, are reluctant to spend longer hours at work unless it deemed necessary.

The next chapter will discuss in more details the subject of work and its relationship to employment in general.

2- **Learning:** The learning activity is an ongoing one. It takes place at work, at home, at the marketplace and virtually everywhere. However, it is common to see nationals spending, after work, few hours between reading, watching educational programs on TV and most recently browsing the Internet in an effort for their learning enhancement.

3- **Social:** The social activity is usually done after working hours where social gatherings are arranged. However, most of the social activities take place on weekends, holidays, and vacations and on occasions that warrant the get together. It is worth mentioning that the people of the Arabian Peninsula maintain strong ties with their family members and relatives. They also enjoy good relationships with their friends and neighbors.

4- **Recreational:** It will be reasonable to say that a working man spends 5 to 10 hours weekly on recreational activities such as walking, swimming, playing ball, fishing, etc.

5- **Religious:** Any worship activities such as prayers and attending lectures or lessons conducted in mosques or in designated places are considered religious activities. Needless to say, that all Muslim adults are required to perform their prayers five times daily. They are encouraged to do so in groups and on a timely basis.

RESOURCES

As indicated earlier, organizations are after the 'resources' of the human resources when it comes to employment. The resources that man individually or collectively acquires or possesses is his means, when put to use, to earning his living. Of course, the more resources an individual has, the better he is in today's job market. There are five kinds of resources that an individual can have. Some individuals possess all these **resources**, at different levels and degrees, while others have only one or more of these resources.

1- **Education:** Academic education is a very important resource. In the Peninsula, education is readily available and free-of-charge. It is made available for all nationals from elementary to university level. In recent years, high demands were for university graduates such as engineers and business majors. Currently, the demand has somewhat shifted toward technicians and craftsmen.

2- **Knowledge and Experience:** Job knowledge and work experience are very precious resources. This is true for both the employee and the employer, as the employer always seeks those who know how to do the job.

3- **Skills and Language:** Skills that are required to do a job such as calculation, reading, writing and communication are also important. The English Language is becoming the business language of the Peninsula. In order to find a good paying job in the business organizations, one needs to be fluent in both spoken and written English.

4- **Personal Qualities:** These are the qualities that are mainly associated with the individual's personality and level of intelligence. It refers to the resources that one inherits or learns from his family. In the Peninsula, *personal contacts* are also a useful resource for one to have. It is common for people to help one another in any way that they can. To get things done promptly or to assist in finding jobs are means widely used among nationals. This sort of attitude towards help is not limited to people of the same tribe or background. It is very much possible to find someone you know taking the extra mile to extend his assistance if asked.

5- **Health and wealth:** Health is a resource that everyone must have in order to find and maintain a job. No matter how educated or experienced the individual is, if he has problems with his health, he will most likely have a problem with his work performance. Wealth, on the other hand, influences the kind of work the individual is willing to do and the type of job he is willing to fill.

SUMMARY

An introduction of the human resources of the Arabian Peninsula is the subject of chapter two. I started by explaining the difference between human resources and the work force. I have stated that the human resources include the elderly, the juveniles, the women and the men (total population) while the work force is only a segment of the human resources. It includes only those who are willing, able and available to work.

This chapter focused on the male segment of the work force, which I referred to as the 'manpower'. As in the case of organizations, the national manpower has its own objectives, activities, and resources, which are summarized in the following table:

OBJECTIVES	ACTIVITIES	RESOURCES
Independence	Work	Education
Raising a family	Learning	Knowledge & experience
Owning properties	Social	Skills & language
Improving living standard	Recreational	Personal Qualities
Leaving a legacy	Religious	Health & Wealth

EMPLOYMENT

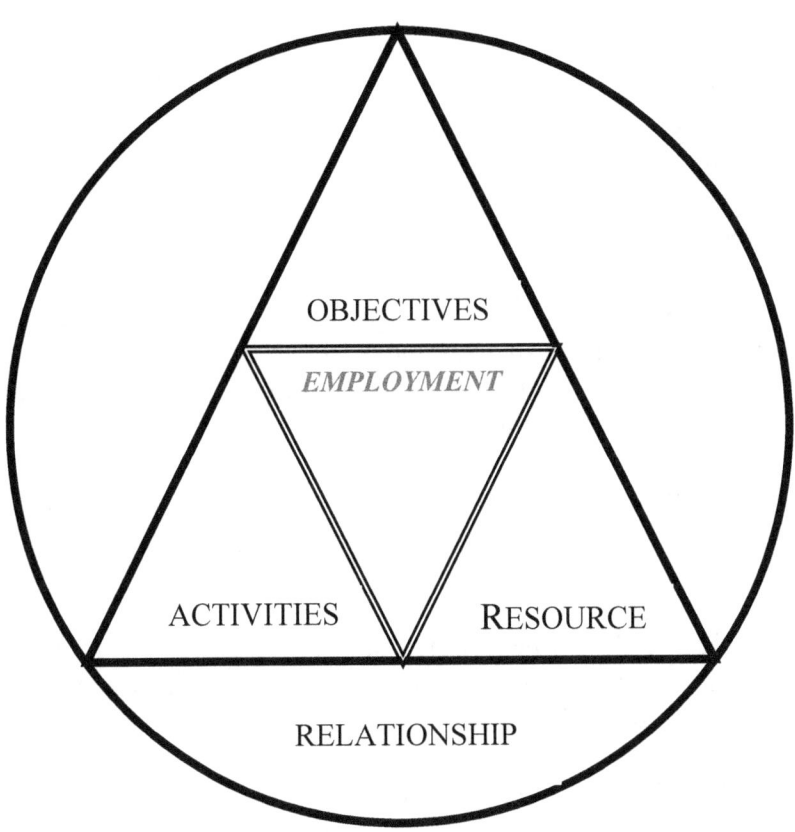

CHAPTER 3

Employment

In the previous two chapters, the private sector and the manpower were discussed. The link between the two is employment, which is the core of this chapter. However, it should be noted that work per se is not limited to employment only. There are also other types of work that people do. The types of **work** can be categorized as follows:

1- **Compulsory:** Any work that the individual is forced to do or must perform. An example will be the compulsory military service in some countries. In the Arabian Peninsula the military service is not compulsory.

2- **Voluntary:** Is quite the opposite of the compulsory work. It refers to any work that people are willing and wanting to do for others at no charge.

3- **Personal:** Is where individuals do things for themselves, their families, and close relatives. It is basically done without financial rewards or gain.

4- **Employment:** Any work performed for financial gain. This is what we do in the form of a job to earn money and provide for our beloved ones and ourselves.

It can be clearly noted that employment is part of man's working activities. Employment is, in essence, the means by which both the organizations and the work force accomplish their own objectives. It is the mutual interest of the employee and the employer.

Nevertheless, in order for jobs to be done appropriately and efficiently, the job objectives, activities and resources should also be identified.

OBJECTIVES

General **objectives** of the jobs we perform fall within these five categories:

1- **Process and Produce:** This is when the job is mainly involved in the processing and/or producing of goods and services such as food, water, fuel, gases, entertainment, etc.

2- **Repair and Maintain:** This is meant for maintaining and/or fixing things. It is basically the maintenance line of the business. The objective here is to ensure that things are working as originally designed.

3- **Treat and Control:** The aims here are to cure beings and/or to purify substances, to control the behavior of someone or something or to change the condition of same.

4- **Commute and Communicate:** In this category, the objective is related to transporting of beings or things to and from places. It also pertains to the information, education, and communication aspect of jobs.

5- **Improve and Develop:** The purpose of the job here is to improve and or develop things that assist the growing process of people, animals, and plants.

ACTIVITIES

The main objectives of the jobs have been pointed out thus far. The activity one performs in the form of duties and tasks constitutes his job. For that, it is advantageous to illustrate the types of such activities that are performed in a given job:

1- **Manual:** Is a physical activity performed by hands or feet. It is known to be the laborers' work.

2- **Mental:** Is where the job is mainly dependent on the work of the mind. They are the intellectual and the creative works of human beings.

3- **Technical:** Is related to the nature of work that is mostly done by craftsmen, technicians, and engineers. It is a combination of both the mind and the body working together in order to accomplish a desired objective.

4- **Administrative:** Is when office and clerical activities are the dominant features of the job.

5- **Systematic:** Is where mechanization and automation are the major activities of the job. Systematic activity is mainly a mechanical one. It usually applies to mass production and any goods that need to be produced on a large scale.

In the Peninsula, jobs are also categorized as professional or non-professional depending on the skills, level of education and experience the job requires. For the purpose of simplicity, table 3.1 illustrates the jobs categories in relation to job activities.

Job Categories

Table 3.1

Non-professional	Semi-professional	Professional	Senior professional
Unskilled	Semi-skilled	Skilled	Highly skilled
Below high school	High school	College degree	University degree
Minimum experience	Some experience	Experienced	Highly experienced
Mainly manual	Mixed	Technical/Admin.	Mainly mental

RESOURCES

The overall objectives and activities of the jobs were explained. It is clear that jobs are not done haphazardly and that everything has a purpose. However, in order for someone to do his job, certain resources must be available to him. These **resources** are listed below:

1- **Energy:** Is one of the most required resources. It could be mechanical, electrical, nuclear, or solar energy or a combination of all.

2- **Time and Place:** All jobs need and must have a place and time that is allocated for it. These resources can be very costly if not wisely utilized.

3- **Instruments and Equipment:** Certain jobs require certain tools, instruments, machines, earth moving equipment and so on, in order to get the job done.

4- **Material and Programs:** These resources refer to the raw materials and programs that are needed for the job. PC programs are a good example.

5- **Manuals and Aids:** Almost everything we buy these days comes with a manual. Just open the box and there it is. There are different types of manuals. Some are operating manuals, while others are designed for repairs. Also, in some cases, job aids are required. A flashing light when repairing roads is considered a job aid.

SUMMARY

There are four different types of work. There is the compulsory work, the voluntary work, the personal work and the employment work (job) that we do for a living. This chapter centers on employment. It defines the objectives, the activities and the resources of the jobs in general as the following table illustrates.

OBJECTIVES	ACTIVITIES	RESOURCES
Process & Produce	Manual	Energy
Repair & Maintain	Mental	Time & Place
Treat & Control & Communicate	Technical Administrative	Instrument & Equipment. Commute Material & Programs
Improve & Develop	Systematic	Manuals & Aids

Part II

THE INFLUENCING FACTORS

VARIABLES

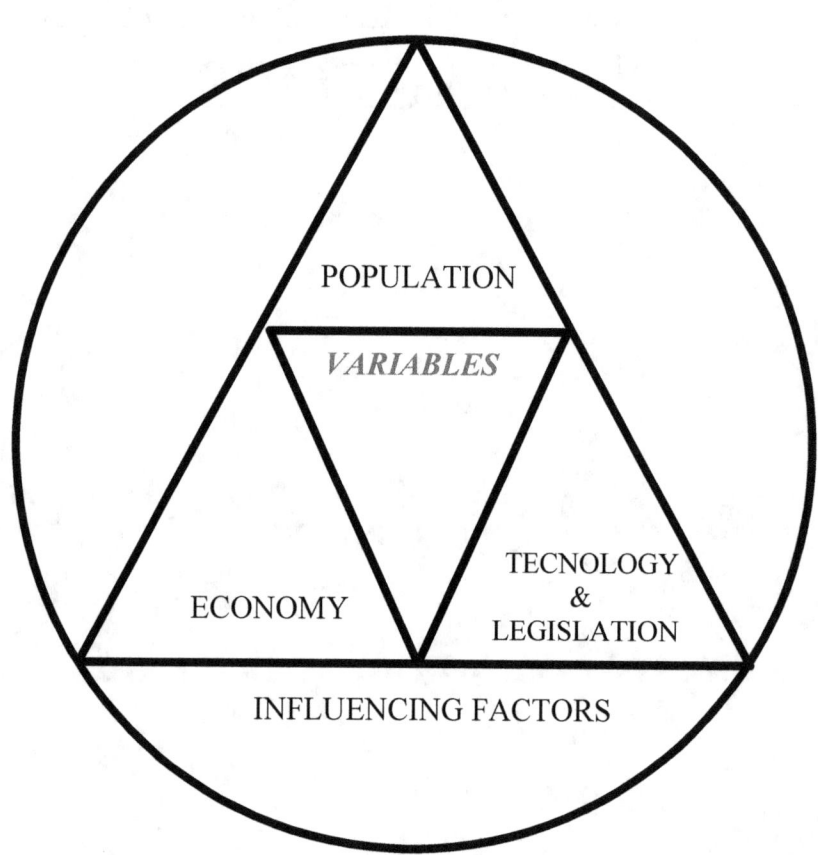

CHAPTER 4

Variables

The planet earth is constantly moving. Our day and night and the four seasons are the result of such movement. The cosmos is based on the law of movement and not stagnation. Movement brings change and change is what makes things different. Changes can take a slow or a fast pace. Let us remember that not noticing change doesn't mean it is not taking place.

This chapter deals with changes in the Peninsula. Population, economy, and technology & legislation are the three **variables** that can greatly influence the status of manpower at a given time.

Population

A growth in the population is indeed a growth in the human resources. The current Peninsula's growth rate is any where between 1.59 percent (UAE) to3.43 percent (Oman). The average growth rate is 2.52 percent, which is considered among the highest in the world. For example, the rate of population increase in the United States is 0.91 percent and in France is 0.38 percent.

The total population of the Peninsula (excluding Yemen) is over 31 million. The point is that the human resources of the nations within the Peninsula are growing and so is the manpower.

When the situation is such that the population growth outpaces job creation, two things happen: unemployment increases, and wages decrease. This is the trend in the Peninsula especially if expatriates are not replaced by nationals. It is simply the law of supply and demand. Unlike twenty years ago, the nation's supply of manpower is not scarce. Of course, this is a general statement as there is still a scarcity of manpower for jobs that either require 'high tech' knowledge and skills or require none and hence are very low in income and status. Population is one variable factor that can affect the manpower and their wages. The other factor is the economy.

Economy

It is no secret that the Peninsula's economy is more or less dependent on oil revenue (production and prices). This has been the case since oil was discovered in 1938. I recall that prior to the oil prices boom in 1973, nationals would perform practically any work that was available at the time, in order to earn their living. Today nationals are more selective in terms of jobs. This is mainly due to the fact that the economy then was nowhere close to where it is today.

What happened in 1973 that made the difference? Well, the price of oil rose from US $2.90 per barrel (September) to US $11.65 (December). This is a little over 400 percent. Again in 1979 another hike took place whereby the prices rose from $13 to $34 per barrel. This represented another 382 percent increase. This unusual change in the growth of economy generated a surplus budget. Such funds were invested in developing the Peninsula. This development had created thousands of jobs in a relatively short period of time. The jobs outpaced the available work force. The demand for nationals exceeded the supply and as a result, their wages went up.

The whole episode was not a normal one. Now things are stable and so is the economy. One should take that into consideration when applying for a job. The economical growth is, no doubt, very influential when it comes to the job market.

Also, we should not forget the economical cycles where there are periods of prosperity followed by periods of depression. In between there are also recessions. These ups and downs in the economy are realities as is life itself.

Technology & Legislation

Technology is the third factor that influences the manpower. It is so obvious how technology has and still is affecting our lives. At times it makes you wonder whether you can cope with the ever-changing technology. There is no need to go back in time and compare situations and conditions. Let us just take the PC that we use in the offices and at home as an example of a fast-developing technology. First there was the 286 types then 386 then 486 and now 586 or 'Pentium'. All this took place in the past ten years or so. Amazing, isn't it? What will it be ten years from today? Only God knows.

Having machines or instruments requires someone with the necessary skills to operate and maintain same. Having up-dated or up-graded ones also requires up-dating skills and knowledge. It is a never-ending cycle.

Having faster and better equipment, machinery and advanced control systems and programs can also substitute labor. This change creates demands for a different type of manpower, as different skills will be needed. The demand will be for manpower that is as sophisticated as the machine itself.

The Arabian Peninsula is known to adapt the latest technology in its industries. To be employable nowadays, one should be on top of the latest trends and issues in the world of technology.

Legislation, on the other hand, can also be instrumental in influencing the status of the manpower. The Labor and Workmen Law and the Expatriates Recruitment Law are prime examples of such legislation. Imposing legislation on work performance; for example, can change the behavior of the individual worker from poor performance to fair or even outstanding performance. Restricting expatriates from performing certain jobs or reducing the number of work visas can shift demands and affect costs.

SUMMARY

Population, economy, and technology & legislation are the three major influencing factors that affect the nation's manpower. Changes in any of these factors will lead to changes in the manpower. Depending on the factor and the type of change, wages fluctuate.

The Peninsula's population is on the rise and so is its manpower. Job creations have been somewhat limited. In addition, the economical growth is now stable and steady compared to the 1970's and 80's. The days of the abnormal economical booms are bygone. Technology is at its best and keeps on evolving. The law of supply and demand is prevailing.

Legislation is a tool that the states and the organizations can use to achieve desired results.

Nationals are challenged by these changes to be flexible in terms of job pay, locations and status. It is also a clear indication that replacing expatriates is only a matter of time.

ENVIRONMENT

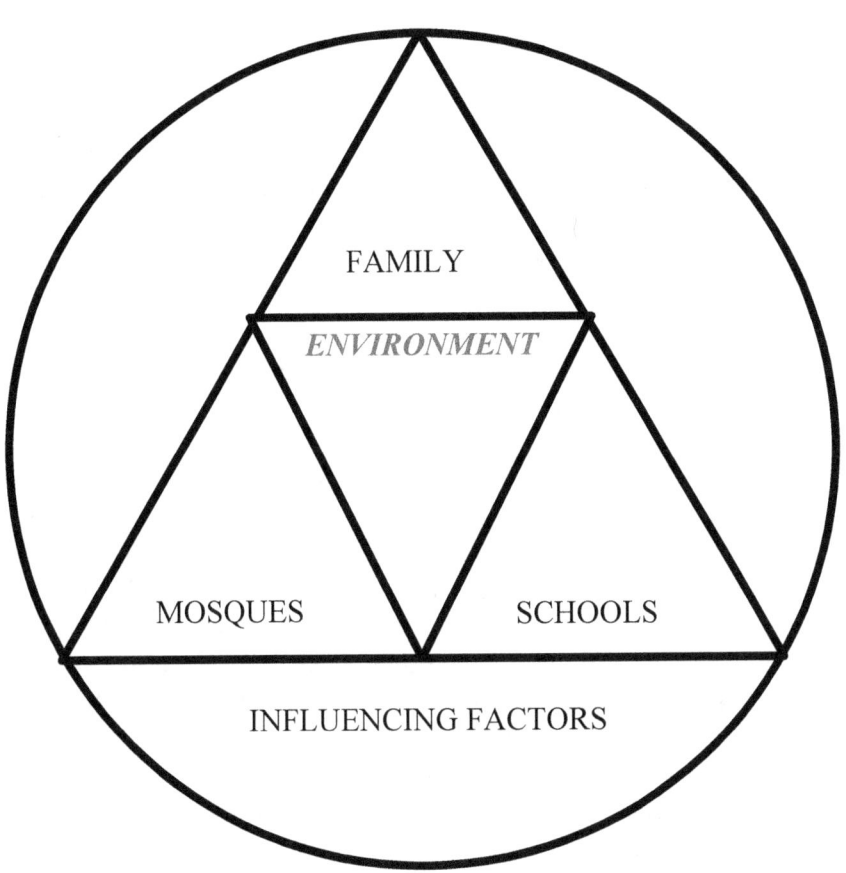

CHAPTER 5

Environment

Man is a product of his environment. What he is today did not happen overnight. It is a complex process that man went through which made him what he is; as complex as his environment. This chapter focuses on the environment and its relationship to man.

There are three basic sources that influence the individual's way of life and thinking.

1- **Family:** When a child is about two years old you give him a candy bar. He will most likely peel off the paper cover, throw the paper on the floor and put the candy in his mouth. Now the question is who will pick up that piece of paper from the floor and place it in the trash container? That person could be the housemaid, or maybe the mother. Teaching that child to clean up his mess, pick up after himself, wash his hands, brush his teeth, and put his toys where they belong after he finishes is, in essence, teaching him how to work and to be somewhat independent. It is also teaching him how to be disciplined. Instilling such qualities in a person begins at childhood by his family and close relatives. A child observing his older brothers and sisters as well as his parents' attitudes toward work and their struggle in life, has a great influence in shaping his personality and developing his behavior.

As children grow older, more responsibility can be added. For example, have the kid wash his father's car (instead of the driver), clean his bicycle or make up his own bed. During summer holidays, more challenging responsibilities can be presented to the children, especially at the adolescent stage. They can work at the neighborhood supermarket or nearest gas station. Incentives are not a problem. I am sure that youngsters have many needs that can be satisfied by earning extra money. It must be clear that the objective here is not money, but rather to teach the youth the value of work and the value of money. For those who can afford to take their vacations during the summer, they can still do so and yet provide a working opportunity for their youth.

What many families do today is spoil their children. They buy them cell phones and encourage them to drive a car while they are too young to appreciate the risks involved. They buy them vehicles instead of having them earn one, not knowing that such action can only lead the children to be irresponsible.

Also, families can help by being less demanding of their youth as they begin to hold jobs. For one to keep taking time off work to do things for the family that can wait seems to be a never-ending process.

Having said that, there are two major elements that influence the family's behavior, which in turn influence the child. One is the family's values and the other is their social status and *income*. A family that tends to have strong work values raise their children to have similar values. Families with low incomes tend to develop responsible children, as they will be required to work at an earlier age in order to help make ends meet.

Also, the people that we interact with influence our lives. They are our neighbors, friends and everyone surrounding us. Their views and values are also very important to us. They represent the society and the network of our interactions. Societies that encourage hard work can only produce members of high working standards and ethics.

2- **Mosques:** When you visit a mosque, you will find people from the ages of six to over sixty. Every Friday there is a speech (Khutbah) where issues of importance are addressed. When children are required to attend prayers at the mosque on a timely manner and sit for the Khutbah, they are being taught order and punctuality. In addition, we are preparing them to be responsible and obedient.

3- **Schools:** Another important source of influence is the school. This is where people spend a good portion of their lives gaining knowledge and receiving an education. At the school age, children are very much influenced by the educational system. Elements that make this system are mainly the *teachers, the curriculum, the syllabus and the facilities.*

I recall that when I was in junior high school, during the Cleanliness Week, all students including myself were requested by the school principal to clean our classrooms. Each had to bring from his home a broom and sometimes a water bucket to help in the mass cleaning of the entire school. In doing so, the school had instilled in us not only the value of work, but teamwork as well. It also taught us humility and the desire to be clean. Needless to say, most of us were looking forward to that day of the year as it gave us a study break, which was our incentive at the time.

The value of work, the importance of earning a living and coping with life after graduation should be mandatory subjects taught at school. Sense of belonging to the nation and its land and the role expected of us as citizens should also be communicated and never be overlooked.

The vocational and training centers are other types of schools. Meeting the requirements of industries is a key element of having a readily available national work force.

The Arabian Peninsula is undergoing an industrial revolution, experiencing both cultural and future shocks. As a result, new sets of values and ethics are emerging. Work values are becoming more and more demanding of one's life.

SUMMARY

The people that influence children the most are their parents. As they reach the school age, the educational system shares that influence. How and what children are being taught is how and what we want them to be. In their early adulthood, the mosques also become another influencing factor in shaping their lives and forming their beliefs.

'Producing' an effective work force is a complex and a lengthy process. It begins at childhood. It involves parents, relatives, friends, neighbors, teachers, and the material being taught at schools. It is a collective effort coordinated by the state.

VALUES

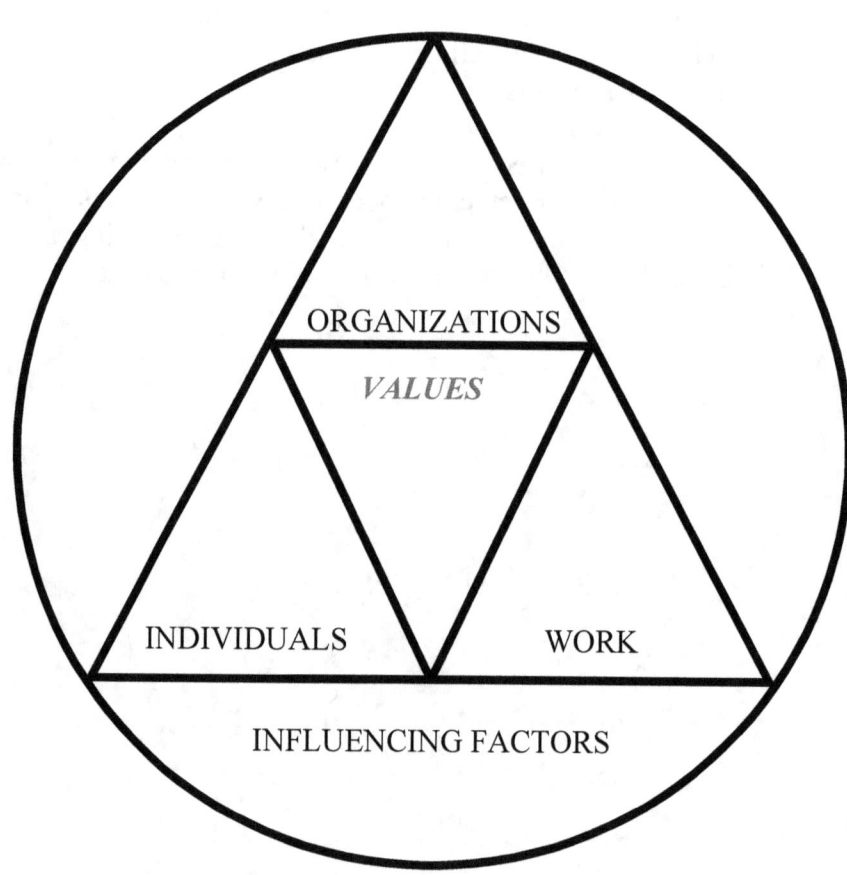

CHAPTER 6

Values

This chapter is devoted to values. Values are understated in the business world today. Yet they dictate our actions and many business decisions that we make. Values need to be addressed and put in the proper prospective. We need to differentiate between values, objectives, and the means to accomplish these objectives. Let there be no confusion. Let us not deviate from the principles of life and our mission on this planet. Let us not turn the 'rat race' into a death race. Look at the world around us today and probe its values and you will wonder no more.

I was reading a recently published book called 'Reengineering Management' written by James Champy where he stated: "Values are the link between emotion and behavior, the connection between what we feel and what we do". Furthermore, he added: "That is where values are, at the crossroads between decency and sound profits". I say it is time we reengineer our way of so called 'civilized' thinking.

Furthermore, social scientists have come to the conclusion that religion teaches values and beliefs and that money is a medium of exchange. I have yet to learn of a religion that teaches greed as its values.

Social scientists have also categorized values into six kinds as: 1) Theoretical 2) Economical 3) Artistical 4) Social 5) Political and 6) Religious. Later on, personal and work values were added. These are in addition to the common values among the human race such as strength, wealth, cleanliness, knowledge, etc.

On the other hand, business organizations, especially in the industrialized nations, dwell on mainly work and social values that are related to work performance and productivity. They published a well-selected set of values to suite their needs. These values are usually published along with the vision and mission statements and are called "common values" or "core values". They are all related, in one way or another, to the bottom line i.e. profit. I ask myself, is money a value or a mean? Is it the purchasing power or a power one should purchase? Do we work for money per se or for what money can do for us?

Business organizations want to appease the owners and stockholders by generating maximum profit. That is fine. I realize that these organizations can't survive on love or some ancient values, nor am I suggesting same. I am asking, in an effort to provoke our thoughts; what comes after profit? How far are we willing to go for the sake of maximizing profit? And how much profit is considered acceptable according to the so-called business values?

One can argue that growth comes after profit. My response to this is what comes after growth and what follows? The point I am making is that improving the bottom line and increasing the value of shares at the Stock Exchange, as important as it can be, still remain to be one of the overall business objectives and in no way is the core purpose of exciting. We should have reasons for the growth and beyond. I say those reasons should reflect perpetual values that can guide us in the ever-tempting world of capitalism. Values for the organizations, the individuals and for the work that we do.

Organizations

Organizations' values are those that can be associated with values of work and linked to the benefits of the society in which they belong to and to the nation under whose jurisdiction they operate. (After all, aren't these organizations utilizing the nation's resources and whatever assistance that is being provided by the state?). Those values can take one form or more of the following:

1- **Social Development:** Any contribution that an organization makes to the betterment of the society and its members is considered to be a value. Developmental requirements and needs differ from one society to the next and from one nation to the other. The contributions should be directed to meet the local needs. Contribution in the improvement or development of the educational system, medical, recreational, transportation and communication facilities are good example.

2- **Economic Development:** Organizations should value any activity that increases the gross national product and improves the standard of living. Investing on projects that produce goods and services should be given priority. Making "money" investments especially in foreign banks does not enhance local productivity. By investing money in foreign banks, we are helping them to produce and ourselves to consume. Our local consumption should be balanced with that of our local production.

3- **Job Creation:** When establishing the business, creating jobs for nationals is one of the most important values. Expansion and growth of existing organizations that don't entail additional jobs are not part of this value. Unfortunately, what we see today is job demolition and not creation. The worst part about this is the fact that it is being done, in most cases, not because the organizations are not making a profit, but on the contrary. The phenomenon of "downsizing", in most cases, is the result of the reengineering process, which I am not against. I often wonder why reengineering is associated with reduction of manpower instead of adding or at least maintaining the same number of people. Why don't they expand their market whereby they can sustain their work force? Why is it that reengineering is always done from inside out and not from outside in?

4- **Value Creation:** It is a value to add values to the goods and services that are being offered to the customers. Customers should get their money's worth. Multi-purpose products are becoming the thing in the marketplace nowadays. Creating values and educating customers of these values are two of the best practices that organizations are competing for in today's business.

5- **Environment Protection:** Many organizations are not interested in protecting their environment while others profess that they care. Needless to say, there are always those organizations that merely meet the environmental regulations and standards set by the state just to avoid penalties and undesired consequences. This should not be the case. I am addressing the issue of <u>wanting</u> to protect the environment we live in and wisely utilizing, not abusing, its resources. Action should be taken because we value Mother Nature, not because we fear legislation. This is what values are all about.

Individuals

In the Peninsula people are known to practice values that are taught by Islam. As a matter of fact, *Islam emphasizes that we are a nation that lives on this planet to work, not work to live.*

For the purpose of this book, I shall focus on those Islamic values that are related to the subject matter. They are as follows:

1- **Fulfillment (Wafa)**: Almost all nations provide free education to their people up to a high school level. Some even provide college education at minimum fees. I don't know of any countries other than those in the Arabian Peninsula that pay their students to go to college. This is in addition to the free lodging, textbooks and subsidized meals at the campus cafeteria.

Years ago, while I was attending high school, both myself, and all other out of town students would receive a monthly allowance to help pay expenses. The point here is that at that time, the state paid the students even at the high school level. These are only a few of the privileges that we as nationals enjoy. For these we are indebted and feel obligated to show our appreciation to our nation.

Learning from an expatriate and replacing him by doing the work at the same level of proficiency, if not better, is paying our dues to the nation. It is a fulfilling value.

2- **Trust (Amana)**: Performing your job as directed, coming to work and leaving on schedule are how an individual earns the trust of his employer. Accepting responsibility and blames for mistakes we commit instead of blaming others is being a trustworthy person. Getting up in the morning to go to work even if we don't feel like it is a trust value.

3- **Sincerity (Ikhlaas)**: Putting our heart at work and paying attention to our job assignments is being sincere. Sharing the working knowledge with co-worker for improvement of the business and not worrying about his taking over our position is a practical demonstration of this value.

4- **Perfection (Itqan)**: This is where we perform our job in a professional manner. We do it to the best of our ability and knowledge. We take the time to do the job right and ask for help when need be. Taking pride in what we do and in how we do it is the value of perfection.

5-**Truthfulness (Sidq)**: Being honest in our dealings with others and most importantly with ourselves is being truthful. Making up excuses for not showing up for work or not doing the work is far from the path of truth.

Work

This is not about work values, but the *value of the work that we do*. Work as we know it consists of certain activities which require certain energies to produce something or to achieve certain results. Results, on the other hand, can be positive (good) or negative (bad). If the results of the work lead or contribute to the quality of life in one of the following areas, then there is meaning in what we do. I say, there is value in the work that is being done.

1- **Safety and Security**: When the end result of our work provides safety or security to the people and or their properties.

2- **Satisfaction and Comfort**: Where the focus of our working activities leads to satisfying the needs of human beings whether they are spiritual, intellectual, physical, or psychological. Also, any work that provides comfort at home, at the workplace, when traveling and virtually everywhere is valuable. The artwork that brings joy and happiness to our lives is a justified value.

3- **Health and Protection**: The work of doctors, nurses, and the entire medical staff. It is also the work of researchers and scientists whose efforts are directed toward the well being of people and their protection from diseases and potential danger.

4- **Peace and Harmony**: The work of peace among people and nations is a vital value of our work. Even wars that resulted in lasting and just peace are considered work that people should value.

5- **Justice**: The work whereby justice and fairness are being imposed is another value of the working activities.

I would like to conclude that wisdom is often a disregarded competency in the business world of today. *Wise management is one who can achieve a status of balance in matters of importance. Values are the tools of wisdom.*

SUMMARY

People are increasingly placing more and more values on materialistic things. Money and profit are becoming in itself the objectives instead of the means. We are living in a tempting world where principles are secondary when it comes to financial gains.

Values influence people's actions and control their behaviors. Values are the driving force behind what people do.

Organizations also have values but need to be more directed toward their employees and to the people in their society. The work we perform should be meaningful and contribute to the quality of life.

The listed values are considered as principal values that should be referred to as a guide for the organization, the individuals, and their work.

ORGANIZATION	INDIVIDUAL	WORK
Social Development	Fulfillment	Safety & Security
Economic Development	Trust	Satisfaction & Comfort
Job Creation	Sincerity	Health & Protection
Value Creation	Perfection	Peace & Harmony
Environment Protection	Truthfulness	Justice

Part III

THE PRACTICAL LOOK

EXPATRIATES

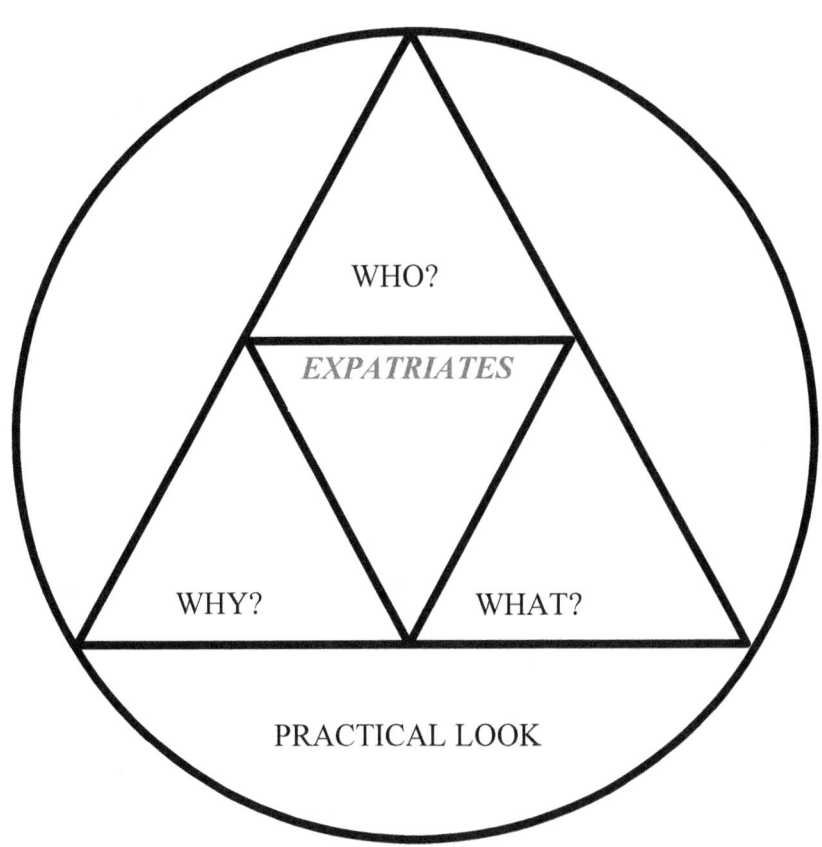

CHAPTER 7

Expatriates

This chapter addresses the **expatriate** work force employed by the private sector in the Arabian Peninsula. Who are they? Why are they here and what do they do? What is their working and living conditions? What are the implications and influences?

Who are they?

I would like to begin by giving a concise background on the movement of expatriates in the Arabian Peninsula during the past three decades.

Prior to the economical boom of the early seventies, the expatriates were lower in numbers in comparison to those of today. Most of them were from the Arab countries and from within the states of the Peninsula. For example, most of the expatriate workers in Saudi Arabia were from the regions of Yemen and Oman. Other Arab nationals came from neighboring countries, such as Palestine, Sudan, Egypt and Jordan.

However, during those days, due to a sudden and huge development, demand for an additional work force rose. At that time, workers were recruited from virtually all over the world except from Communist countries. The Koreans and the Turkish played a major role in Saudi Arabia, especially in the establishment of its infrastructure. When most of the major projects were completed and during the recession years, the demand shifted for a more economical manpower. This is when Asians were hired in bigger numbers.

Today, the non - Arab Asians represent the majority of expatriates. They are estimated to be in the region of 10 million people working in the Peninsula (excluding Yemen). This is more than 30 percent of the total population. The remaining expatriates are either from Western countries or the Middle East.

As a result of the above, the following questions are mainly related to the Asian work force.

Why are they here and what do they do?

During my career I have not come across an expatriate who is not here for the money. It may not be the only reason, but it is definitely the number one incentive. Acquiring international experience as well as learning new technologies are other incentives.

Let there be no mistake. I am not undermining the role that the expatriates have played in the development of the Peninsula. Nor of the sincere efforts and contributions made by most of them during the years. I am putting forward issues of concern that exist now, which did not exist before. Changing environment calls for changing roles. The new role of the expatriates is to work themselves out of jobs by helping nationals take over.

At any rate, the majority of the Asian expatriates are performing labor, semi-skilled and skilled work. They can be easily located at construction sites and can also be seen in shops and supermarkets handling the sales and delivery activities. Most of the janitorial and cleaning jobs are handled by them. There are others that are holding professional jobs as well.

What is their working and living conditions?

Most of the expatriates working in the private sector come here on single status contracts, especially those engaged in non-professional jobs.

Leaving their families, wives, and children behind, they take the journey to the land of opportunity. Some even pay money to the recruiting agents in their home country in order to be employed. It may be OK to do so when you have money that you can spare.

But the reality in most cases is that they borrow, sell things or mortgage their properties in order to get the job. That is desperation.

Furthermore, the majority of these expatriates sign a three-year contract with one paid airline ticket. If they wish to take an earlier vacation, they have to manage on their own. By visiting their living quarters, you will note that, on the average, three to four people share one 4x4 meter room. They also share the responsibility of their cooking and housekeeping. However, there are companies that provide their workers with mess facilities in the camp or at the workplace.

Their work schedule averages 9 hours per day and 6 to 6.5 days per week (with no overtime payment claiming that it is included in the package for those who work more than 8 hours). Their salaries, depending on nationality and profession, vary anywhere from US $ 150 to $ 1500 per Gregorian month (in Saudi Arabia 60 percent of the expatriates employed by the private sector earn less than SR 900.00 or US $ 240.00). Paying employees on time does not always happen. Unfortunately, it is a common practice of some employers to pay a month or two later.

It is no wonder that many organizations of the private sector are reluctant to go for the nationals. On the surface, it seems to be very economically attractive to hold on to the expatriates even if nationals are available to do the same job.

It will come as no surprise to find some expatriates going around looking for cars to wash or yards to clean after their working hours. Since the income they receive is insufficient, they find it necessary to earn extra money.

What are the implications?

Having a non-indigenous work force is not in itself a problem. Industrialized nations are well known to have expatriates in their work force both legally and illegally. For instance, the US has Mexicans and others doing laborer work. Germany on the other hand, employs a good number of expatriates mainly Turkish (estimated 4 million expatriates) and France employs North Africans and so on.

However, the issue, in the Arabian Peninsula is somewhat different. For one, the number of expatriates is rather high when compared to the total working population and at the same time natives are becoming unemployed.

Furthermore, there are other concerns that cannot be neglected such as:

Technology Transfer and Beyond

If nationals are unemployed or not fully participating in the nation's development process, how can technology be effectively transferred to the minds and hearts of the people?

Transferring technology is our responsibility and no one else's. We cannot and should not expect the expatriates to simply spoon-feed us their knowledge - the knowledge that took them years of blood, sweat and tears to acquire.

Acquiring up-to-date knowledge is only the beginning of our mission in this life. Working with the expatriates and learning their technology is a prerequisite to creating our own. We ought to build on their technology just like the western societies built their civilization on ancient Arab inventions. We can accomplish this by work and work only.

Security and Social Risks

Organizations who rely heavily on expatriates are being vulnerable. What happens if those who know the business decided not to renew their contracts and leave work? What impact would this have on the business? It is true that nationals can also leave. However, the difference here is that the know-how would remain within the boundaries of the Peninsula. Another difference is that the ties between nationals would ensure a separation that is most satisfactory to both parties. I don't see the possibility of taking revenge in case of disputes that can jeopardize the business or hinder the national interest.

Another risk is a social one. There are about 200 nationalities from all over working in the Peninsula with diversified traditions, cultures, and religions. This represents a serious social impact and possibilities of spreading crimes of different kinds.

Inertia and Lethargy

Again, relying on expatriates to do the bulk of the work can only encourage the upcoming generations to be dependent, if not lazy. The future generations need to witness, experience, and observe the people of our time being active and productive. What we do today will set the standards of tomorrow. The practice of sponsoring expatriates or foreign investors to do business in the Peninsula while the sponsor is merely inactive is another form of inertia. At times, it may be a lucrative business or an easy income to providing just sponsorship, but it is not work and hence contribution to the society becomes waning and too limited.

Economic Cycle and burden

As indicated earlier, the expatriates are here mainly for monetary gain. It is estimated that, on an average, 50% of their income is being remitted to their home country. The annual remittance in the Gulf Courtiers is estimated at US$ 20 billion per annum. (In Saudi Arabia alone, the expatriates' home remittance averages US$10 billion). If this fund is spent or invested in our country; it would generate more economic growth and activities, which will lead to more job opportunities for the nationals. This is not to mention the development that such cycles can create, which, will in turn benefit the business organizations.

Also having a great number of expatriates that consume and take advantage of the subsidized goods and services, which are intended for nationals, can only increase the country's burden and costs.

Unemployment

Unemployment takes place when people who are willing, able and available to work can't find jobs. Unemployment creates free time and leads to poverty. The combination of these two in any given society invites immoral behavior and corruption. Beside how would an unemployed young man be expected to get married and raise a family if he has no job? What would that do to the young unmarried women who are waiting for that big event? It can only lead to more corruption.

In the Peninsula, the problem is not that there are no jobs in the market, but no market for nationals. This is another implication of relying on an expatriate work force.

I will be closing this chapter by quoting an article I have read in the Middle East Expatriate Newsletter of May 1996. It says: "Unemployment among UAE nationals is more than 15%. This is double that of America and eight times greater than the European average. And the problem will continue while there is excessive reliance on Asian and other foreigners, according to a local study." The article went on to state "The bitter fact is that the main reason for the unemployment problem in the UAE is the imbalance in the wage system because of the private sector's policies of dependence on cheap labors."

SUMMARY

The expatriate presence in the Peninsula is dependent on the need for them. This need could be the result of shortage of indigenous work force, lack of know-how or both. The number of expatriates required is also calculated on those grounds. Economics play a role in determining the origins the expatriates are to be recruited from.

As things change at the host country or at the home country, the number of expatriates needed and or the origins also change.

At present the national work force is not scarce and the know-how is not a problem that can't be resolved. Yet the number of expatriates is higher today than ever before. Having expatriates working and nationals unemployed is a trade-off that can only have negative implications. One needs to re-evaluate the situation and recalculate his economics.

Expatriates have helped build our nation. There is no denying the fact. In the past years, they have contributed to the development and the prosperity of the country. Now is the time for the indigenous work force to take charge, not only in leading positions, but also in all jobs. To build for tomorrow one should start today.

REQUIREMENTS

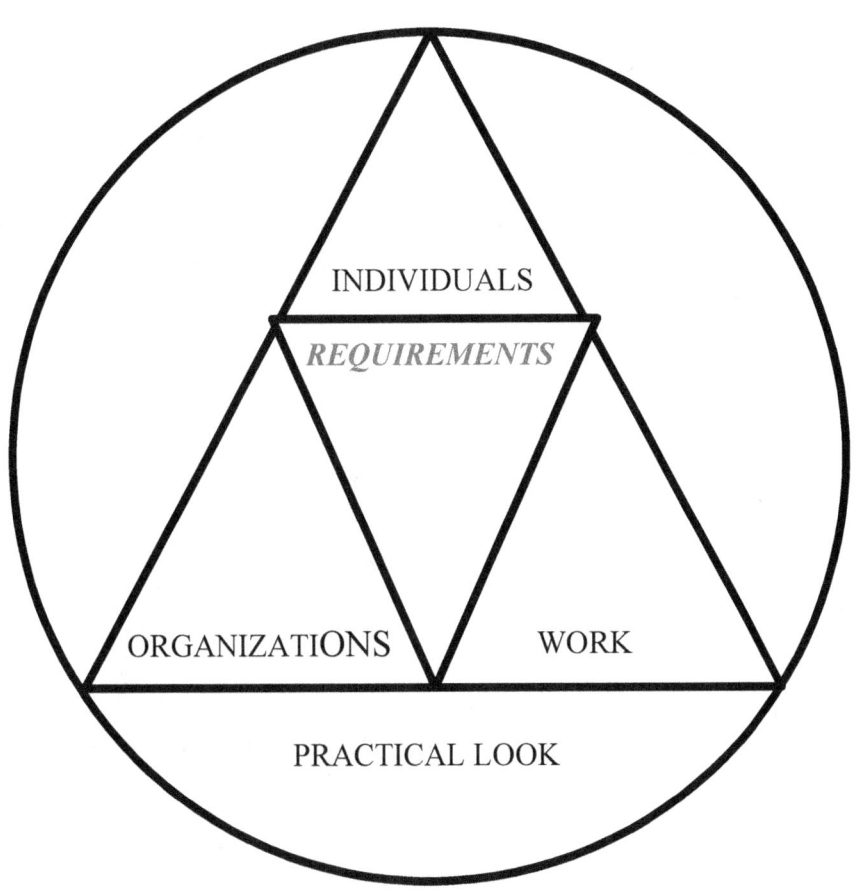

CHAPTER 8

Requirements

This chapter deals with the requirements of the individual, the private sector and that of work when it comes to employment. When requirements of all parties are met, then a satisfactory relationship is established, and the contract becomes genuinely binding.

The Individual

In order for the individual to play his role in having an effective indigenous manpower in the region, he should understand and meet the requirements of the organization, the employer. Five fundamental requirements that the employer seeks from his employees are identified below:

1- **Knowledge and Skills:** Knowledge required performing the job and the skills needed are the first things the employer would scrutinize at the time of recruitment. Job knowledge is a combination of both theoretical knowledge (academic education and classroom sessions) and practical knowledge (on-the-job training and work experience). Skills are also learned and require practice. There are basic skills such as reading, writing, calculating, etc. and there are specific skills, which mainly refer to the "level of dexterity" that one should posses in a particular job or profession. So, for employers to insist on having qualified personnel, they are no doubt aiming to reduce the training cost and the mistakes associated with performing the job.

2- **Cost Effectiveness:** This is another item on the private sector's agenda. This is where economics come into the picture.

How much will this individual cost the organization? Is hiring an expatriate worker less costly than an indigenous one? These questions, and others like them come to mind. For one thing, hiring costs depend on the nationality of the expatriate. Also, it depends on how the calculations are done. Supply and demand at the marketplace and whether or not you want to minimize your training costs are also major elements. Chapter 9 deals with the cost analysis pertaining to this issue.

3- **Performance and Ethics:** Private sector demand high performance from their employees. This is understood as they are competing against the world-as it is the case today with all of the profit-oriented organizations. Therefore, good performance on the job and productivity are key elements to success. They are also the base for salary increases (merit) and job promotions. The high competition also demands employees to be creative and innovative at their work. Also, one's attitude toward work and colleagues at the workplace is very important. Attendance and punctuality are too an indication of one's good work ethics.

4- **Reliability and Dedications:** Many private sector organizations fear that having nationals is having somewhat unreliable employees in their work force. The employers need to feel that their instructions are being followed and the job is being done. Taking off work, not showing up for work and not following things through is very much disturbing to the business. Therefore, employers seek employees that are most dedicated to their jobs-those who come to work on time and their social life obligations don't interfere with the business. Those who go to sleep early and don't spend most of their night, before a working day socializing, are in demand.

5- **Loyalty and Flexibility:** Loyalty to the firm is very much desired during one's employment. However, being flexible is definitely a more demanding competency that the organization looks for. Flexibility in terms of doing what is requested from the employee and not necessarily what is stipulated in his job description. Most importantly being flexible in working at locations that may not be desirable and working longer hours as required from time to time.

The Organization

Organizations should also play their roles if an effective indigenous work force is ever to take place. It is the employer who is going to utilize the services of the employee. This is where the buck stops. Therefore, it is imperative for the organization to understand and appreciate nationals' needs and requirements. Five major requirements that nationals demand as far as employment is concerned have been identified. These requirements among the nationals are common and do not differ much from those of the industrialized nations. The degree of which an organization is willing to meet such requirements reflects its contribution in achieving this goal.

1- **Job Satisfaction:** The national tends to be selective of the job he is going to perform. For instance, college graduates are keen to look for jobs that agree with their studies and fields of specialty. Less educated people tend to be more flexible, especially in recent years. However, they will not apply for jobs that are not acceptable to the society at this time, such as plumbers, barbers, bakers, caterers, gas station attendants and janitors. In general, nationals prefer administrative and office work rather than fieldwork. However, it has been realized lately that the job market for such positions is saturated. Also, it has been realized that managerial posts are limited and that the demand in the marketplace is shifting to other professions.

2- **Pay and Benefits:** A good compensation and benefits package is another requirement that the nationals try to attain. Base salary, transportation and housing allowances, medical and dental care for him and his dependents are key elements to accepting or rejecting a job offer. For those who are already working, a competitive package is a major factor for retaining employees in the organization. Also, organizations in remote areas or those offering temporary jobs should compensate by offering a somewhat higher than average package in order to attract employees.

3- **Training and Career Development:** Almost all newly college graduates and non-experienced persons have training and development on their minds when searching for jobs. Employers who offer training and on the job progressions would definitely have the preference. However, the nationals tend to be more ambitious and eager for job advancements when compared to others of the industrialized nations. They simply have higher expectations. Organizations can patiently orient those eager ones that gaining job knowledge is a time-consuming process which has to be done right and should take its pace.

4- **Work Environment and Condition:** Safety at work, reasonable working hours, office work and work location closest to home are most desired when nationals are seeking employment. As far as work location is concerned, nationals are becoming less persistent especially for those migrating from villages to the big cities.

5- **Job Security and Job Respect:** These are very important employee requirements. In most cases, nationals would compromise on pay, if need be, provided that they feel secure in their jobs and that employers are treating them with respect and dignity. The fact that nationals feel secure has been their main motive behind working in the public and semi-private sectors. This is in addition to the less demanding work and reasonable working hours at the public sector.

The work

So far, we have learned what the organizations require from the individuals and vice versa. Meeting these requirements at the time of employment is a good start. However, it is definitely not good enough to maintain a long, lasting and mutually beneficial relationship. This is simply due to the fact that change is a natural law. Organizations and individuals change and so circumstances, conditions, and priorities. Therefore, employees and employers should always touch base with the work requirements. By doing so, they will be in a better position to overcome any potential differences and reduce unpleasant surprises.

To keep the wheel rolling, there are five main requirements that work demands from both the organizations and the individuals. Meeting these requirements is dependent upon the situation and varies from one organization to the next. The same applies to individuals. These requirements are to be met long as they don't hinder the core values and the main objectives of the organization, individual and work.

1- **Compromise:** Surely organizations and individuals alike have to compromise from time to time. Why? Because it is a work requirement. They could compromise on pay, benefits, working hours and the like. Organizations also compromise in their business dealings with the state, suppliers and clients for the sake of work.

2- **Relocation:** Organizations move their locations and hence individuals working there will be relocated. It could also mean that the individual is requested to relocate to another place, city or even country - be it temporary or permanent with his family or without.

3- **Change:** This is when the organizations change their work activities in part or in whole. As a result, employees are affected. It also applies to employees who need to change their behavior, attitude or even their career in order to stay working.

4- **Investment:** Investment is a must and an ongoing process. Organizations invest in businesses as well as in people. Similarly, at times employees need to invest for enhancing their knowledge and skills.

5- **Efficiency:** Good workmanship is an important work requirement. Whatever organizations or individuals do it must be done in an effective and timely manner. To be efficient, one must struggle his way through the working life.

SUMMARY

To have an effective and a productive working relationship between employees and employers, mutual benefits should be the base. If both parties are not benefiting in a balanced manner, this relationship will not last. To ensure that both parties are mutually benefiting, their requirements must continuously be met. To do that one should first know, understand, and appreciate the requirements of the other including work. This will lead to satisfaction and in turn to prosperity for all concerned.

The following summarizes the subject requirements:

EMPLOYEE	EMPLOYER	WORK
Job satisfaction	Knowledge and Skills	Compromise
Pay and Benefits	Cost Effectiveness	Relocation
Training and Development	Performance and Ethics	Change
Work Environment And condition	Reliability and Dedications	Investment
Job Security and Job Respect	Loyalty and Flexibility	Efficiency

INVESTMENT

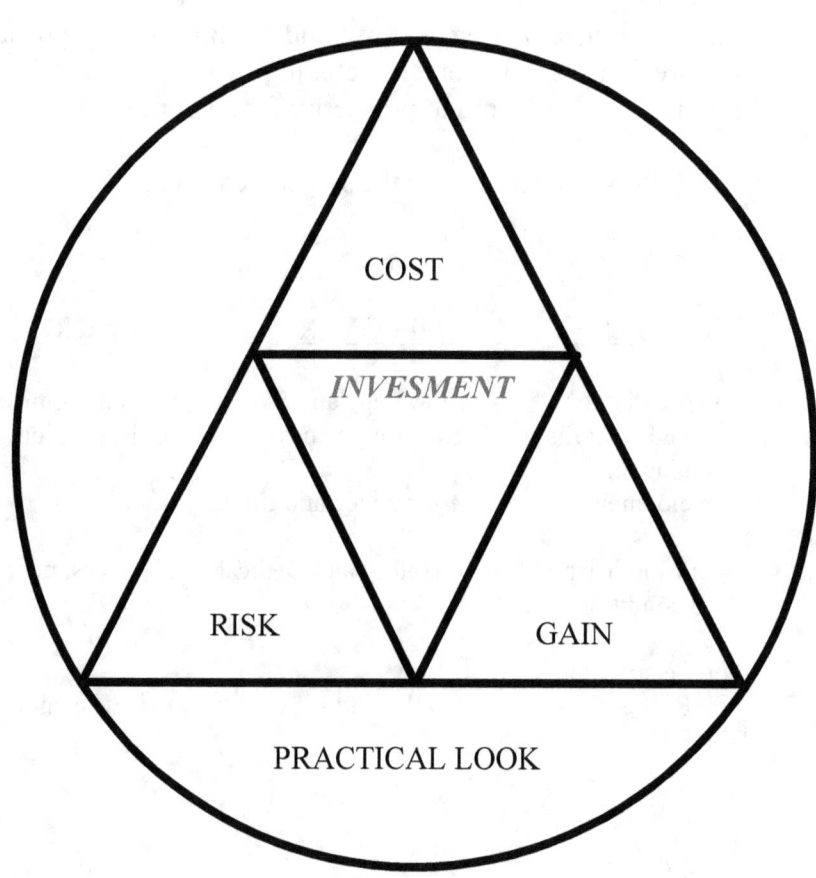

CHAPTER 9

Investment

No doubt minimizing costs and maximizing revenues are day-to-day management activities and concerns. What most organizations do when it comes to human resources is to take the traditional approach of hiring at the least cost. There is nothing wrong with that approach provided that the least cost employees are mostly indigenous. But to keep hiring expatriates, is called 'management by illusion'. It is a shortsighted approach. Unless you are in business for a short period, you can't afford to keep on doing that.

Many organizations realize the need for a stable, competent and motivated work force in order to achieve their business objectives. That is why they value their employees and invest in them. They invest in their real assets- the driving force behind success.

Therefore, this chapter will deal with **investment.** Not in machines or real estate but in people; the indigenous manpower.

There are three dimensions to investment. They are known to everyone and are simple. *Cost* is the first dimension - you need to spend money to make money. The second one is the *risk* involved, as there are always risks associated with any investment. The third dimension is the expected return on investment - your *gain*.

Cost

How much does it cost to recruit, retain, and repatriate an expatriate vs. a national? The following tables illustrate the costs, in 1997, for three different incumbents as follows:

Table 9.1

Job Title   : Driver
Job Category   : Non-Professional - Experienced
Working Hours   : 10 hours per day/ 6 days per week
Contract duration   : 3 years (expatriate - single status)
                       1 year (National - married status)

Item	Asian (Indian)	National
Base Salary	1,920.00	4,800.00
Overtime @ 1.5	000.00	780.00
Housing @ 25%	480.00	1,200.00
Transportation @10%	000.00	000.00
Meal	480.00	000.00
Other	000.00	000.00
Residency fees	160.00	000.00
Medical @ 7.5% **	200.00	750.00
GOSI/ Insurance	45.00	560.00
Vacation	80.00	200.00
Air ticket (Round trip)	160.00	000.00
Sub Total (1)	3,525.00	8,290.00
Recruiting fees	150.00	000.00
Ticket- initial posting	500.00	000.00
Driver's license	20.00	000.00
Merit program @ 5%	228.00	240.00
Administrative @ 10%	192.00	480.00
End of service	560.00	540.00
Ticket- final repatriation	560.00	000.00
Sub Total (2)	2,210/6*= 368.00	1,260.00
Grand Total (1+2)	3,893.00	9,550.00

Costs in US $ per year
* Expected years of service in the organization
** Minimum $ 200.00 for expatriate and $750 for national

Table 9.2

Job Title   : Technician
Job Category   : Semi-Professional - Experienced
Working Hours   : 8 per day/ 6 days per week
Contract duration : 2 years (Expatriate - single status)
                    1 year (National - married status)

Item	Asian (Philippine)	National
Base Salary	4,800.00	12,800.00
Overtime	000.00	000.00
Housing @ 25%	1,200.00	3,200.00
Transportation 10%	480.00	1,280.00
Meal	000.00	000.00
Other	000.00	000.00
Residency fees	160.00	000.00
Medical @ 7.5%**	360.00	960.00
GOSI/ Insurance	112.00	1,493.00
Vacation Pay	200.00	535.00
Air ticket	440.00	000.00
Sub Total (1)	7,752.00	20, 268.00
Recruiting fees	150.00	000.00
Ticket- initial posting	665.00	000.00
Driver's license	20.00	000.00
Merit program @ 5%	480.00	640.00
Administrative @ 10%	480.00	1,280.00
Ticket- final repatriation.	665.00	000.00
End of service	2,160.00	720.00
Sub Total (2)	4,620/4*= 1,155.00	2,640.00
Grand Total (1+2)	8,907.00	22,908.00

Costs in US $ per year
* Expected years of service in the organization
** Minimum $ 200.00 for expatriate and $ 750 for national

Table 9.3

Job Title   : Engineer
Job Category   : Professional - Experienced
Working Hours   : 8 hours per day/ 6 days per week
Contract duration : 2 years (Expatriate - married status)
                    1 year (National - married status)

Item	Asian (Indian)	National
Base Salary	9,600.00	24,000.00
Overtime	000.00	000.00
Housing @ 25%	2,400.00	6,000.00
Transportation @ 10%	960.00	2,400.00
Meal	000.00	000.00
Other	000.00	000.00
Residency fees	160.00	000.00
Medical @ 7.5% **	720.00	1,800.00
GOSI/ Insurance	224.00	2,800.00
Vacation Pay	400.00	1,000.00
Air ticket (Annual)	480.00	000.00
Sub Total (1)	14,944.00	38,000.00
Recruiting fees	250.00	000.00
Ticket- initial posting	840.00	000.00
Driver's license	20.00	000.00
Merit program @5%	1,968.00	1,200.00
Administrative @ 10%	192.00	480.00
Ticket- final repatriation.	840.00	000.00
End of service	3,780.00	1,350.00
Sub Total (2)	7,890/6*=1,315.00	3,030.00
Grand Total (1+2)	16,259.00	41,030.00

Costs in US $ per year
* Expected years of service in the organization
** Minimum $ 200 for expatriate and $750 for national

In comparing the cost of employing an experienced Asian expatriate versus an experienced national for the same job, it is noted that the national would cost, on average, two and a half times more than an expatriate (these figures will be reversed when compared with other expatriates from Western Europe or USA). This is true for professional and non-professional jobs alike. This is basically the cost of the investment provided that the subject nationals are readily available at the labor market. In the case where training is needed to enhance the national's qualifications, the cost is illustrated in table 9.4 as follows:

Table 9.4
Training cost in US $ for a technician incumbent
(Industrial high school graduate)

Element	Under Training				Under Employment
	English for (3) months	Vocational for (3) months	OJT For (6) months	Total	
Base Salary	1600.00	2000.00	4800.00	8400.00	
Overtime	000.00	000.00	000.00	000.00	
Housing	400.00	500.00	1200.00	2100.00	
Transport	160.00	200.00	480.00	840.00	
Medical	188.00	188.00	480.00	856.00	
GOSI/ Insurance	000.00	000.00	000.00	000.00	
Vacation	375.00	375.00	750.00	1500.00	
Training/Supervision	5000.00	5000.00	1000.00	11000.00	
Administrative	160.00	200.00	480.00	840.00	
Total	7883.00	8463.00	9190.00	**25,536.00**	Per year 22,908.00*

OJT: On -the -Job Training
*Refer to Table 9.2

One can conclude that the total cost (training + wage) to qualify an indigenous graduate for a technician's job is US $ 25,536.00 that is almost the same as employing an experienced one. Therefore, it would not make much sense to elect the training option unless a qualified technician is not available. Also, it can be noted that the highest cost endured is limited to the year of training. This is where the organization pays an expatriate to do the job while also paying for training a national. Upon completion of training and repatriating the expatriate worker, the amount of US $ 22,908.00 is reduced to US $ 14,001.00 per annum, which represents the difference in wages between the national vs. the expatriate.

It should be stated that the above quoted training cost is based on producing non-advanced technicians for non-sophisticated jobs and for one year of training. There are cases where the training period is less than one year while others require longer than one year. There are also different training methods and approaches. To reduce the training period and in return reduce costs, some companies combined the English training with that of the Vocational while others combined Vocational with the OJT.

Another important element is that all training costs should be amortized on the number of years that the national is expected to serve the organization instead of expensing it in one fiscal year.

Risk

The cost of the investment is now known. The risks involved in proceeding with such investment are also as important to know. Therefore, let us identify these risks in order of concern.

1- Employee commitment: The employee, after completing his training, may leave the organization for a better income, location and or working hours (he could simply leave, now that he is trained!). Or the employee may work for a relatively short period of time and then leave the organization. One cannot expect organizations to keep training nationals only for them to leave. They are not in the training business.

2- Employee performance and productivity: The national may not perform as good as the expatriate. Productivity may also be reduced as a result of the replacement.

3- Employee attendance and reliability: A national employee has too many social commitments and obligations. His taking time off work to attend to some of these obligations will disturb the business. I am sure you have heard these statements before: He is a good worker, but his attendance is terrible. He hardly comes to work. I can't relay on him.

These are some of the main concerns that employers have when it comes to hiring nationals. These represent the risks organizations are reluctant to take. It is not to say that all these concerns are merely allegations nor that there are no risks involved in any business endeavor. Nevertheless, these risks can be minimized and dealt with. Selection is the key tool to minimizing the risk. Another tool will be the contract that the individual will sign prior to joining the organization. Holding back on the trainee's original certificates or some of his income as a long-term savings for him can be made part of the employment contract. These and other similar tools can apply if the situation warrants such actions and if the organization feels more secure in doing so. I find that the most effective tool is winning the employee's heart. Proper induction, coaching and care can perform miracles.

Gain

The costs and the risks have been calculated and identified. Now the gain that is expected from this investment will make or break the deal- any deal.

Some companies don't see much benefit in employing nationals. What they see are higher operating costs, lower productivity and more day-to-day employees' grievances and headaches. One may ask: Are you proposing that there are benefits in employing nationals? Yes. There are.
The gain is not a short term one and it takes more than just money to achieve a desired gain. You are paying for the potential output not for actual. In addition, I wish to quote Jerre L. Stead, the former Chairman and Chief Executive Officer of AT&T Global Information Solutions. He said in his October 11, 1994, speech, in explaining his "Value Equation" that: "Here is a very important "people power" corollary: The way our associates (meaning employees) treat our customers is, and always will be, a reflection of how we treat our associates. Think about that." In explaining himself he further added: "We work very hard to

engage and "delight" associates- who are then motivated to "delight" our customers. When our customers are delighted, we see profitability grow rapidly. As a result, our company's shareowners are delighted."

So, the end result will be profitability as a number one gain. Another gain will be a further economical growth as you are increasing the spending power of nationals. This is in addition to having a more stable manpower in the organization and less social problems in the region. This is not to mention the principle values discussed in chapter 4 of this book.

SUMMARY

Employing nationals should be looked at as an investment and not a burden to the business. This investment, like any other investments, entails costs, risks, and gain. As most of the nationals will mainly be competing with lower paid workers (Asian expatriates), cost analysis shows that employing a national is two and a half times greater than employing an expatriate of the same discipline and experience. This gap is not caused by the high wages demanded by nationals as much as it is caused by the poor economical condition and taxes of expatriates' home countries.

On the other hand, the risk involved in this investment can be minimized if not eliminated if selections are done right and proper employment contracts and orientations are made.

The gain expected from this investment is initially painful, but worthy. Organizations who invest in their human resources will make the difference not only at a local level, but globally as well. They will be able to achieve financial growth and community recognition.

Part IV

THE REPLACMENT PROGRAM

EVALUATE THE BUSINESS

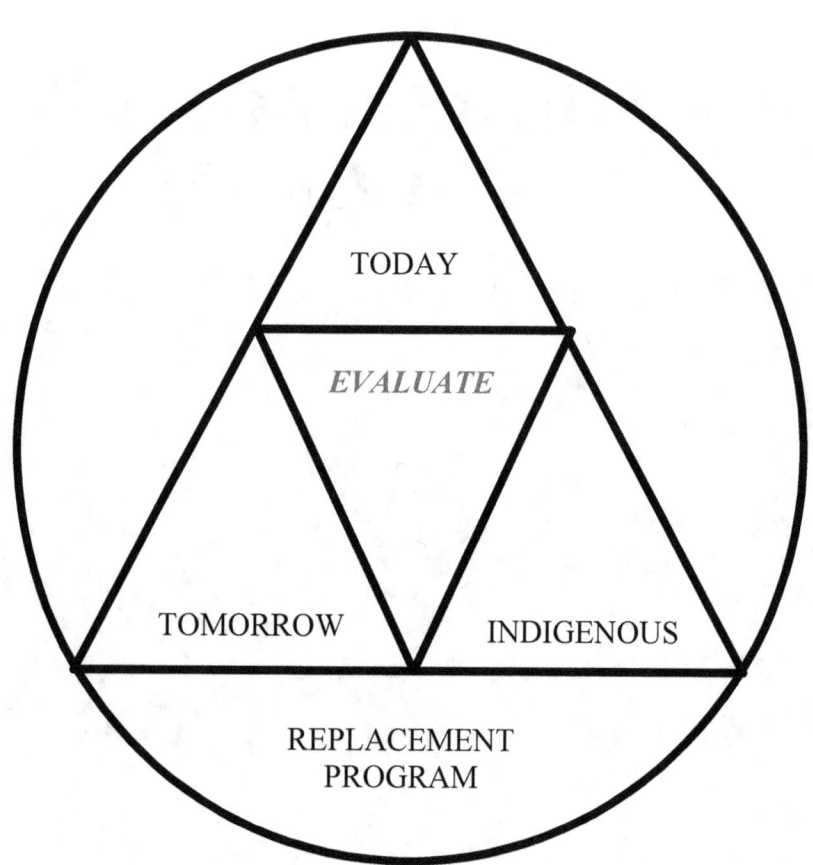

CHAPTER 10

Evaluate the Business

All preceding chapters were necessary to give an in-depth conception of the issues and concerns of having and not having an indigenous work force. A global view of the situations was presented. It is up to us, the individuals, the society, as well as the organizations to make it happen.

We should always remember that we are a nation justly balanced who seek equilibrium in all matters. A temperate people we are. We do not disregard the momentum of profit gain nor ignore the law of economics. Yet, the duties to our fellow man and the commitment to the homeland are not being neglected. To help lead the nation is no simple task. Hard work is a must and determination is the only way.

This chapter is designed to guide you in taking the first step toward the pain of change. From an inferior fortune to a superior gain.

Your expatriate work force is relatively far too many in number and your organization is seriously considering a replacement program. This program is to be implemented in three stages: *evaluation, establishment,* and *execution.* Call it the E approach.

This chapter will guide you through the first stage; that is to **evaluate the business** in its entirety. There is no point in going through a major change in your human resources if your business is shaky to start with. First and foremost, you must evaluate the business. This *evaluation* should be made by high-level management or by a team of experts assigned by top management. This stage is also divided into three steps as follows:

①Evaluate the business as is today.

The objective, in step #1, is to determine the level of satisfaction of:

A- The owners/stockholders- in terms of: 1) investment security 2) profitability 3) growth 4) reliability 5) quality.

B- The customers/ clients- in terms of: 1) quality of your products and services 2) prices 3) delivery time 4) after sale service/warranty/guarantee 5) the value added of your products and services.

C- The employees- in terms of: 1) job satisfaction 2) wage and benefits 3) training and development 4) working environment and condition 5) job security and respect.

If the results of the *evaluation* are favorable, then proceed with the second step. If, on the other hand, the results are not favorable, then you have a problem that could be serious. Such a problem needs to be addressed and resolved prior to making any further commitment. You should identify the exact area in which the dissatisfaction is taking place, since when and why? You should then come up with a remedy.

②Evaluate the business in light of tomorrow.

In step #2 your objective is to envision the status of your business in light of future developments and changes. Say 10 years from today what business opportunities would there be for your organization? Do you see your organization offering new products or services? What resources would you require? What is your research and development unit or department working on? How would these opportunities affect your manpower?

To do a thorough *evaluation,* the following areas should be examined:

A- The resources- in the terms of: 1) human 2) natural 3) capital 4) Produced 5) technology and information.

B- The activities- in the terms of: 1) your products and services cycle 2) competition 3) customers' needs 4) suppliers 5) market trends.

C)- The state- in terms of: 1) government spending 2) economical growth 3) legislation 4) inflation 5) standard of living.

Now that you have a feel for tomorrow, do you see a promising future for your organization? If not, you should reconsider your overall business objectives and activities. You should work on having strategic plans for your organization.

③ Evaluate the business at maximum Indigenous work force.

In step #3, your objective is to tentatively identify changes needed and has an assessment for the costs associated with the replacement program at maximum exposure. Obviously, it will not be possible to achieve the 100% nationalization of your work force, nor is it the intention to do so at present. It is the maximum exposure that needs to be assessed. This can be achieved by identifying all positions that can be nationalized at this time or in the near future. Chapters 11 and 12 contain detailed information in this respect.

The *evaluation* at this point is a rough one. As you approach the *Establish* and the *Execute* stages of the replacement program, a more detailed evaluation will be required. However, for this exercise, the evaluation should cover the following areas:

A)- Costs of 1) Recruitment 2) Wages 3) Training 4) Repatriation of expatriates 5) Administration.

B)- Sources from 1) College graduates 2) Vocational schools 3) High schools 4) Labor market 5) Other industries.

C)- Work 1) Rules 2) Conditions 3) Environment 4) Procedures 5) Methods.

Now how do you see the business? Is the program costly? Are you required to do a lot of changing around to suit your indigenous work force? Was your feasibility study done at the time of your business inception on the basis of having a 100% indigenous work force? If not, what was your estimated percentage? Was that percentage reasonable? Finally, how much will it cost your organization if it does not implement a replacement program?

At this point of time and after the overall evaluation has been completed, you are about to make a very serious business decision. The "moment of truth" has come. All options should be considered. Think ahead and think globally. If results are not promising, consider merging with other organization(s) of similar activities and objectives. Or at least think about synergy and sharing resources with others. Think positive. Think that having part of a strong business is much better that having none.

SUMMARY

A business organization is always required to *evaluate* its performance. A three-dimensional evaluation is rather comprehensive. It reveals the true picture of the organization, shows where you stand in the marketplace and measures your strengths and weaknesses. If the owners, the customers, and employees are satisfied, then you are in business.

To maintain such a business in a competitive and changing world, management should read into the future seeking opportunities for growth and improvement. Merger and integration with other organizations should be seriously considered and perceived as one of those opportunities that can benefit and sustain the business.

Replacing the work force is an upcoming change whether we like it or not. A challenge that can only add to the other challenges that management is already faced with. A challenge that affects one of your most important resources.

ESTABLISH THE PLAN

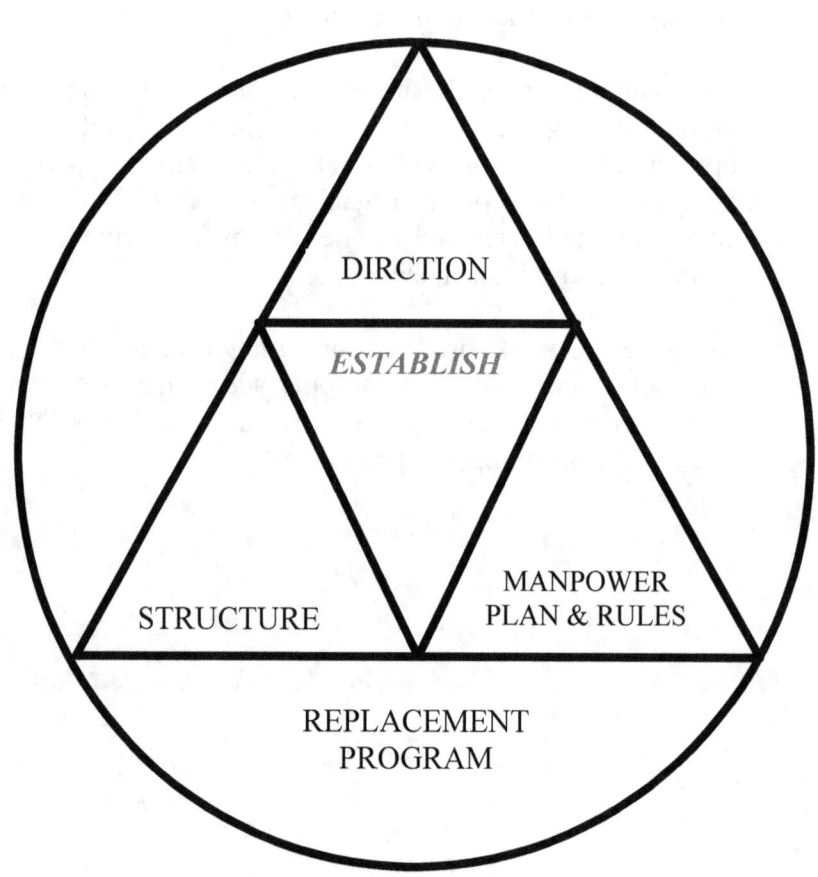

CHAPTER 11

Establish the Plan

In this chapter, I will outline the second stage of your replacement program. This stage requires you to **establish a master plan** based on the evaluation made in the first stage. This plan is divided into three parts as follows:

①Establish the business direction

This part of the master plan includes:

A- The businesses activities: Do you want to maintain the same line of business or change to something else? If you do not want to change, do you intend to make any modification or improvement in your operation process? In which area can you reduce costs? Do you need to change location or open new offices, branches, shops and/or stations? Or maybe condensing is what needs to be done.

If there will be no changes made to your business direction, at least you should focus on improving same. This can be accomplished by 1) minutely examining the process of your work in its totality 2) seriously considering outsourcing activities that are not of a core nature to your business and a non-added value process. Whatever the case may be, it is imperative, at this stage, to have a layout of your new direction.

B- The business resources: Are there any equipment or machines that you can obtain that would have an impact on productivity? What technology is available to your organization that can make a difference to the bottom line? In applying new technologies, is there any reduction or addition to your manpower? How good are your financial resources? Is cash a problem? Whatever it is, you should make every effort to assure maximum utilization of available resources and eliminate waste.

C- The business strategies: How is your organization going to achieve the satisfaction of the owners, customers and employees when performing the activities and utilizing the resources? How are you going to maintain the balance of satisfaction (short and long term)? What are your plans?

②Establish the Organization Structure

Based on *establishing* the business direction, you are able to proceed with the organization restructure. This restructuring is to include the following:

A- The organization chart: All related job activities should be grouped together representing a unit. Related Units together represent a Section and similarly all related Sections are to represent a Department and so on. Having that in mind set your Organization Structure using minimum supervision as possible (7 to 8 workers reporting to one leader). The Organization Chart is important to have. It shows the Span of Control and Chain of Command. <u>It is also required for your headcount purposes.</u> Table 11.1 below illustrates a chart of a Unit in the Maintenance Department.

Table 11.1 Organization Chart

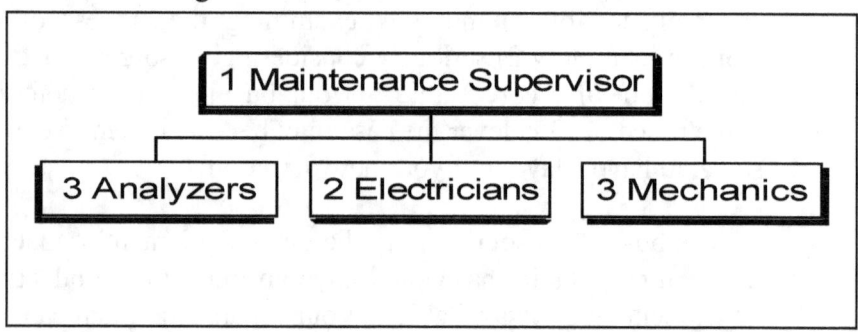

B- The job analysis: Each job indicated in the organization chart should be analyzed and as a result, you will have job descriptions and job specifications. <u>This is required for your training purposes.</u> As a specimen, see Table 11.2.

Table 11.2 Job Analysis

Incumbent name: xxxxxxx	Position: HR Manager
Immediate supervisor: xxxxxxx	Position: CEO
Section: xxxxxxx Department: Executive	Location: xxxxxx

PART I- Job Description

Purpose of the job: To manage the employees' recruitment, training and remuneration function in line with company strategies and objectives.

Regular duties	% of time
1) To ensure that Personnel Policies and Procedures are intact	25%
2) To ensure that training and development programs are intact	25%
3) To ensure the Manpower and Succession Plans are intact	20%
4) To ensure that the Remuneration Package is competitive	15%
5) To handle employees grievances and disputes	15%

PART II- Job Specification

Educational Requirement/ Equivalent: University degree in Business Administration or Law degree.
Prior Experience Required: 10 years experience in Employee Relations and Personnel Administration. Last 4 years in leading position.
Specialized Skills or Knowledge: English language- knowledge in PC and the Labor Law. Good supervisory skills and analytical ability, innovative and forward thinking.
Number of direct reports: 7   Financial Authority: US $ 10,000.00
Working Condition: Mainly office   Physical Requirement: N/A
Working Hours per day: 8   Per Week: 48 Overtime: N/A

Incumbent's Signature: --------------------------- Date: -------
Supervisor's Signature: --------------------------- Date: -------
Approved By: -------------------------------------- Date: -------

C- The job classification schedule (JCS): A group of jobs are to be assigned to a grade and each grade is to correspond to a salary. Each salary will have a minimum, a median and a maximum amount that the organization is willing to pay for that job. *Establishing* a salary structure requires conducting a salary survey and job evaluation with similar organizations in your region. Make sure that the JCS has a career structure for nationals. JCS is required for your hiring purposes. For an example, see Table 11.3.

Table 11.3 Job Classification Schedule*

Job Title	Salary Grade	Minimum	Mid-Point	Maximum
Clerk I Driver I	2	$ 300.00	375.00	450.00
Electrician Mechanic Clerk II Driver II	3	$ 345.00	430.00	540.00
Maintenance Foreman I Senior Electrician Senior Mechanic	4	$ 400.00	495.00	620.00
Maintenance Foreman II Operations. Supervisor	5	$ 460.00	575.00	720.00

*In US$

③ Establish the manpower plan and work rules

The manpower plan

Having established the new organization structure, you should be able to *establish* your manpower plan. The plan should be for a minimum of a 3 to 5 year period and to include:

A- The permanent positions are to be identified and coded separately from those temporary ones. Permanent meaning any job that is essential to the operation of the organization's long-term needs. Permanent positions are those the organization is planning to nationalize. Temporary positions are predetermined, based on work requirement, to be a short period of time and therefore, the organization is not planning to nationalize. If there is a reduction in the work force (headcount) as a result of the evaluation process, expatriates should get the preference for termination.

B- The names and nationalities of your current work force along with any additional requirements of future personnel.

C- The year in which you plan to hire additional employees or terminate the services of unneeded ones. For illustration purposes on manpower plan, see Table 11.4

Table 11.4 Five-year manpower plan 2001-2005

Position- Permanent	2001 V	E	N	2002 V	E	N	2003 V	E	N	2004 V	E	N	2005 V	E	N
CEO		1			1			1			1			1	
Opns. Mgr.	1			1			1			1			1		
Opns. Supr.	2			2			2			0	2		2		
Engineer	1	3	1	1	3	1	1	2	2	1	1	3	0	1	4
Operator	12	2		6	8		0	14			14			14	
Maint. Mgr.	1			1			1			1			1		
Maint. Supr.	2			1	1		1	1		0	2		2		
Maint. Tech.	15	2		10	7		5	12		0	17		17		
HR Mgr.		1			1			1			1			1	
HR Specl.	2			1	1		0	2		2			2		
Clerk	4			2	2		0	4		4			4		
Accountant	1		1	0	2			2		2			2		
Driver	2			2			2			2			2		
Labor	80			80			80			75	5		70	10	
Total	3	121	10	3	105	26	3	90	41	3	76	55	2	71	61
	134			134			134			134			134		
PDEs															
Engineer	1			1			1			0			0		
Accountant	1			0			0			0			0		
HR Specl.	1			1			0			0			0		
Trainees															
Operation	6			6			2			0			0		
Maintenance	6			5			6			0			0		
Total	15			13			9			0			0		
Grand total	149			147			143			134			134		

E= Expatriate   N= National   V= Venture
HR= Human Resources   Maint.= Maintenance
Mgr.= Manager   Opns.= Operations
Supr.= Supervisor   Tech.= Technicians
PDE= Professional Development Employee

Assumptions: a) No training required for clerks and laborers
 b) One year training for Operators, Technicians, HR & Accountant
 c) Two years training for Engineer
 d) Promoting Operator to Supervisor in year 2004
 e) Promoting Technician to Supervisor in year 2002 &04

The work rules

With a work force being mostly indigenous, surely you need to review your work rules, policies and procedures to suit the nationals. This is provided that you already have them in place. If not, now is the time to establish same. These rules, policies and procedures should cover:

A- Working hours (regular working hours not to exceed 8 per day and 6 days per week) and overtime payment. Also shift work administration, if any. Rest day, breaks and prayer time, working hours during Ramadan and the like should be included.

B- Leaves, vacations, medical, and business travel.

C- Penalties and rewards systems.

D- Salary administration such as merit increase and promotions

SUMMARY

Establishing the master plan requires *establishing* the future business direction. This direction is a result of careful examination and study of the business processes, activities and resources in today's world as will as tomorrows.

The master plan also entails adjusting your organization's structure and manpower plan accordingly. Revising job descriptions, job specifications and the job classification schedules are all the byproducts of this plan. Your work rules and the organization's policies and procedures should also be looked at to suit your national work force.

By setting the master plan, you would have actually completed the groundwork of the organization's transformation. Your vision is now translated into a workable and practical plan and your objectives became achievable.

EXECUTE THE PLAN

CHAPTER 12

Execute the Plan

In this chapter, the intention is to **execute the plan** and put it to work. The *execution* process requires management determination and dedication of the team that is being assigned to this task. The focus here is going to be on the *execution* of the part that pertains to manpower. *Execution,* is to be done in the following order:

①**Execute By Hiring The Team Leader**

If the organization does not have a national as Human Resources (HR) Manager who is qualified for this major assignment, then the priority is to hire one. There should be no compromise on qualifications. This is a key position as the success of the whole program is very much dependent on him. If unable to hire one within the targeted time, you may want to consider employing one, on loan, from other organizations such as public (universities) or semiprivate (oil/petrochemical companies). Nevertheless, the HR manager should have a true knowledge of the local culture. He should also be familiar with your type of business and should be made aware of the organization's plans and strategies. Within a reasonable timeframe, the HR manager is expected to achieve the following:

A- To ensure that the organization structure is established and ready for implementation. The same applies to the manpower plan, the work rules and the organization's policies and procedures. If not as yet finalized, the HR manager is expected to do so. If help is required, same is to be sought when and as needed.

B- To ensure that proper budgeting is made, and a necessary fund has been allocated for this program. The same applies to office space, furniture, and equipment, if needed.

C- To ensure that training facilities and programs are available or accessible for those employees that require further training.

②**Execute By Setting Recruitment and replacement Strategies**

The Recruitment Strategy

An analysis should be made to determine the cost-effective approach to hiring nationals. Depending on the supply and demand at your location, you need to decide which is more feasible to hire; experienced, non-experienced workers or both. The following is the process in setting your recruiting strategy:

A- <u>Know your labor market</u>: If you do not have a good feel of the labor market and what is available at your location, you can do the following:
  - Contact your nearby Labor office.
  - Contact your local recruiting agents including "dot com" organizations.
  - Contact colleges, universities and/or technical institutes.
  - Place an advertisement in your local newspapers. Also consider online advertisements.

Furthermore, the following guidelines will give a general idea of what to expect in terms of the indigenous labor market sorted by job category. (More information is available in Chapter 3) Each category has a scale of one to three. The higher the number is the better your chances are in finding readily available, willing and able nationals to do the job:

I) Non-professional jobs: These jobs require minimal or no skills, experience, and education. The pay is low and working hours are long. Mainly jobs under scale 3 are socially acceptable at this time.

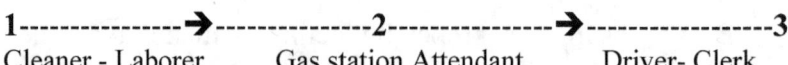

1----------------➔---------------2----------------➔-----------------3
Cleaner - Laborer   Gas station Attendant   Driver- Clerk

II) **Semi-professional jobs:** These jobs require some degree of skills, experience, and education (High school more or less). The pay is some- what reasonable and so are the working hours. Jobs under scale 2&3 are socially acceptable.

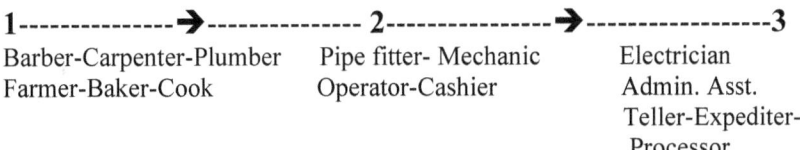

1----------------➔---------------- 2----------------➔----------------3
Barber-Carpenter-Plumber   Pipe fitter- Mechanic   Electrician
Farmer-Baker-Cook   Operator-Cashier   Admin. Asst.
                                                   Teller-Expediter-
                                                   Processor

III) **Professional jobs:** These jobs require skills and college education and experience. The pay and working hours are reasonable. Jobs under scale 2&3 are socially encouraged.

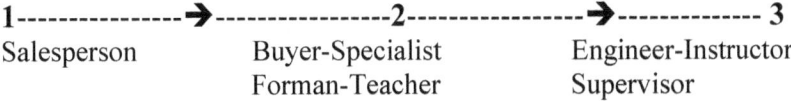

1----------------➔----------------2----------------➔-------------- 3
Salesperson   Buyer-Specialist   Engineer-Instructor
                   Forman-Teacher   Supervisor

IV) **Senior professional Jobs:** These jobs require high skills, global experience, and university education. All Jobs under this category are socially acceptable. However, readily available candidates are questionable.

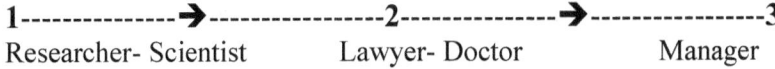

1---------------➔-----------------2---------------➔----------------3
Researcher- Scientist   Lawyer- Doctor   Manager

B- <u>Know your training:</u> There are two things that should be known. The first one is the training facilities available to your organization and their related costs. The second one is the training needs of your work force.

- Training facilities: If your organization is not equipped with the required training facilities, you should then contact: a) Your local chamber of commerce, b) Training organizations; in order to collect information on the type of training available, timing and costs.

- Training needs: If training needs have not been identified and prepared, then you can do so by sorting the candidate's qualifications and competencies and comparing them with the job analysis (already prepared). The gap, if any, between the individual's current qualifications and what the job dictates are your training needs. In doing so, you will be asking yourself: What additional competencies and skills does the employee/candidate need to bring him up to standard so he can perform the job effectively and with minimum supervision? You have to do that for each individual. Once training needs have been identified, you should then consult with the training people to determine appropriate training programs.

C- <u>Know your selection</u>: Go for positions that the market can supply. Try to stick to your region and start with hiring those who are living closest to your work location. Look for those with good working ethics and skills to minimize training costs and time. Use a series of tests that are most applicable to your industry and line of business to help you in selecting the best. Use personal interviews with candidates and don't shy a way from asking relevant questions. Once candidates are selected go for a "specified period" employment contract.

The Replacement Strategy

It is obvious that by now your objective is to replace your expatriate work force at the lowest possible cost with the least business interruption. But perhaps what is not obvious at this stage is the anxiety among the expatriates and the rumors that are being created in the organization. This in addition to the informal conflicts, demoralization and low productivity expected during this period of instability and change. Therefore, your strategy should also take that into account to ensure a transition as smooth as possible. In view of this, the following strategy is recommended:

A- To honor the contractual obligations with the expatriates. Unless otherwise stipulated in the employment contract, termination should be made on the contract expiration date with an advanced notice of at least 30 days. Final settlements should be paid in full, on time and as per policy.

B- To allow a grace period for hand over. No matter how much experience newly hired employees have, they still need some time to get acquainted with the organization's system and its culture. However, for those experienced ones, a few weeks will be sufficient for hand over. The non-experienced workers will require a longer period of time. Exact duration is dependent on the qualifications, training needs and on-the-job progression. Therefore, the duration varies anywhere from 3 months to 3 years. To expedite on-the-job training, paying bonuses to those expatriates involved in the training process is worth doing.

C- To replace the expatriates in the following priority:

1- The expatriate that is high in cost versus the national who is readily available and who is qualified to perform the work.

2- The expatriate that is high in cost versus the national who is available but requires some training in order to be fully qualified to handle the job.

3- The expatriate that is low in cost versus the national who is readily available and is qualified to perform the work.

4- The expatriate that is low in cost verses the national who is available but requires training to be fully qualified to perform.

③**Execute By Setting A Succession Plan**

The succession plan is the actual process of implementing the replacement program. It is the final stage for having an indigenous work force in positions they are willing to hold. All the planning done, the surveys conducted, the information collected, and the preparations made will be essential for an effective succession plan. The succession plan and implementation require the following:

A- Sort out the employees who can be promoted first and provide them with the support, guidance, and rewards for assuming additional responsibilities.

B- Sort the candidates in two main categories:

   1- Immediate replacement- no training is required
   2- Deferred replacement - training is required

C- Sort out training venues to be either:

1) On -the -job training, 2) Off -the -job training, 3) Both (1) & (2). In certain positions or for certain disciplines, depending on availability, you may also need to consider out-of-country training.

Now use the manpower plan (which has already been prepared) and incorporate the expected replacement date for each expatriate whose job is subject to replacement.

Updating the manpower and the succession plans is an on-going process. Any time you have successfully completed a replacement of an expatriate, you should up-date your records accordingly.

SUMMARY

Executing the master plan is the third and final stage of the replacement program. It is the implementation of the *established* plans, which were based on your initial and total *evaluation*.

Executing the master plan is a simple process, yet a very important one. Start by hiring the man who is going to take charge of the replacement process. Then focus on the strategies of recruiting the nationals and repatriation of the expatriates.

The link between recruiting nationals and repatriation of expatriates is the succession plan. The succession plan is an implementation process of the manpower plan. The key to effective succession is training and developing the national work force. Minimizing the training costs can be achieved through the good practice of candidates' selection.

Part V

THE KINGDOM OF SAUDI ARABIA

DEVELOPMENT IN FOCUS

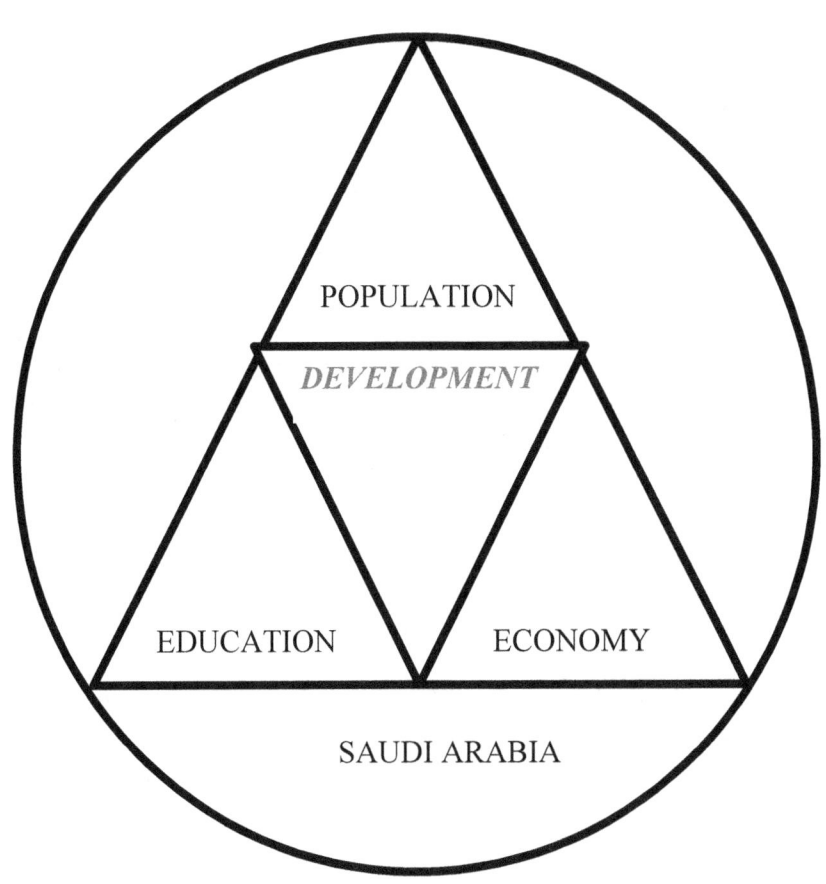

CHAPTER 13

Development in Focus

This chapter, as well as the two that follow, are devoted to the Kingdom of Saudi Arabia.

Since its foundation in 1932, the Kingdom's vision has been to transform the country into a developed nation and yet maintain the Islamic values, traditions, and its unique culture.

This chapter will walk us through some of the substantial achievements and the remarkable developments that have taken place in Saudi Arabia thus far. Knowing that it is rather impossible to cover in few pages the development of three decades, the focus here is going to be on the areas that are relevant to our subject.

Population

The Kingdom of Saudi Arabia is the largest country located on the Arabian Peninsula (there are seven countries in the Arabian Peninsula). It occupies approximately 80 percent of the total area, and the Saudis represents about 47 percent of the total population.

The 2001 estimates revealed that the total population of Saudi Arabia, including expatriates, is almost 23 million. The expatriates are estimated at 6.0 million or 25 percent of the total population. This means approximately 17 million being the Saudi population of the Kingdom.

The Saudi females represent about 45 percent of the population. Therefore, it could be said that there are approximately 7.65

million females and 9.35 million males making the 17 million as the net Saudi population.

The statistics also indicated that 50 percent of the population is under 15 years of age. Those over 65 years old represent approximately 2.6 percent of the total population. The birth rate is 3.7 percent a year and death rate are 0.6 percent. The life expectancy is averaging 68 years.

It is also estimated that the Saudi working males are now about 3.41 million. The 2001 per capita income averages a little less than Saudi Riyal (SR) 28,125 or US $ 7500 and the average family members are five.

By the year 2020 the population is estimated to rise to 29.7 million. One can imagine the future work force of the kingdom. It is apparent that the supply will exceed the demand and hence the wages of the Saudi work force will drop making the recruitment of nationals more attractive.

Expatriates

As indicated earlier, the expatriates are estimated to be in the region of 6.0 million including their families.

Since the Saudization at the public sector is more than 94 percent and fewer than 10 percent in the private sector, the Saudization in the private sector has been activated. This action is deemed necessary to accommodate the upcoming Saudi manpower.

Education

In 1951, when King Fahad was the Education Minister (then Prince Fahad), he made every effort to achieve qualitative education in the kingdom. He was able to establish the long-term education planning. He also succeeded in making education a priority in the government's future projects. It could be said that King Fahad is the founder of the Kingdom's modern education. He was the first Education Minister and was assigned the education portfolio at his request.

At that time the total number of primary schools was 326, with 43,734 students. In 1958, the number of primary schools rose to 9,600 with 95,960 students. In 1970, a greater number of schools were in operation, seven universities were established, and thousands of students were sent abroad for higher education in different fields.

Now the total number of male and female students exceeds 4 million. The number of public schools for males is 11,191. There are 11,441 public schools of various levels throughout the Kingdom, accommodating 2,015,700 female students.
During the fifth five-year plan (1990 -1994), more than SR 153 billion was spent on education (18 percent of the budget). To cope with the rapid population growth, the Ministry of Education has allocated SR 1.7 billion in 1996 for 222 new school projects in addition to the 600 new schools and colleges established for females. Furthermore, SR 900 million has been invested in 220 private schools.

This increase will continue in order to cope with the future population growth. It is estimated that by the year 2020, an additional 22,500 elementary schools be built together with 6,000 intermediate, secondary schools and colleges. Furthermore, we anticipate seeing more private schools and colleges in the region. With the Internet facilities being available, online education will be popular and more students will take advantage of the non-traditional education system.

Economy

In 1968 the kingdom's Gross Domestic Product (GDP) was SR 17 billion. In 1980 it reached the peak of SR 535 billion making an average annual growth of 29 percent. After that it dropped to SR 271 billion in 1985. Then in 1990 it rose to SR 432 billion. In 2001, the GDP was SR 637.5 billion. The growth for the past year was positive, i.e., in 2000, about 4.5 percent. The cost of living has been moderate for quite some years with an exception to 1995 as it rose to about 4.5 percent from less than 1 percent. This sudden increase is clearly due to the changes introduced in January 1995 whereby the prices of petrol and utilities went up.

Furthermore, the 2000 budget run a surplus of US$ 6 billion. The current deficit in the budget is anticipated to disappear in the year 2002.

However, the country and since the Gulf wars, is in the barrowing mode mainly from local banks in the kingdom. The 2001 figures indicated the debt is in the region of US$ 168 billion.

Industries

In the industrial arena, the strategy was to attract businessmen to invest by utilizing available resources. For that the kingdom offered the following:

A- Attractive long and medium term loans. In addition, interest free loans were granted up to 50 percent of the total costs of a newly established project or for expansion or improvement of existing ones. The published data revealed that the loans extended by the Industrial Development Fund exceeded SR 1.7 billion in 1995. When comparing this to 1985 where the loans reached SR 750 million, an average annual growth of 19.1 percent has been achieved during the ten-year period.

B- Tax exemption for ten years for industrial projects and five years for commercial ones provided that the Saudi partner owns a minimum of 25 percent of the equity.

C- Duty exemption for imported raw materials and equipment that are not locally made in the kingdom.

d- Setting up industrial estates with all required facilities and services with utility costs being subsidized. In addition to the industrial cities under Royal Commission for Jubail and Yanbu, there are currently eight other industrial cities in the kingdom covering a total area of 57 million square meters.

D- providing free movement of capital to and from the kingdom.

E- Giving preference to locally produced goods and services for the purchasing requirement of the public sector.

This is in addition to the assistance and services the kingdom is providing such as preparation of feasibility studies.

This action has led to a remarkable economical development in the country. Today, there are thousands of operational industries employing more than thousands of workers.

Currently the private sector contributes about 35 percent to the kingdom's GDP.

The Saudi (Public and Semi- private) industry is divided into three major categories, namely oil refineries (Saudi Aramco), petrochemicals (SABIC) and offshore industries. In the petrochemical industry, Saudi Basic Industries Corporation (SABIC) is playing a dynamic role.

To cope with the latest development and to enhance the private sector investment even further, in April 2002, the kingdom has modified its investment policy whereby it made it more attractive.

Agriculture

The agricultural sector in the kingdom has also bloomed. For example, the output of wheat in 1975 was approximately 3,000 tons. In 1985, it exceeded three million tones. It is worth mentioning that as of 1985, the kingdom has attained self-sufficiency in wheat production.

The agricultural development was not limited to wheat. There was also a tremendous growth in vegetables, dates, citrus fruits, eggs, poultry products, milk and the like. Such development has led to food industries, as is the case of the vegetable oil industries, which started in 1977. By 1995, there were eight vegetable plants with a total investment of SR 470 million and a production of 290 thousand tones.

In recognition of the great achievements of the kingdom's agriculture development, the UN's Food and Agriculture Organization (FAO) has awarded the kingdom an international merit certificate.

Currently agriculture contributes about 5.3 percent to the kingdom's GDP. As the agricultural sector matures, food subsidies are to be ceased. In 1991, the kingdom started a gradual decrease of subsidizing food.

Banks

Like other sectors, banks have also progressed throughout the years to meet the country's growing demand. Today, there are 11 commercial banks in kingdom. Saudi Arabian Monetary Agency (SAMA) is the Saudi central bank. National Commercial Bank (NCB) is the largest bank in terms of assets.

To maintain a competitive advantage, automated teller machines, credit cards and installment borrowing have become the norm among these banks. Recently online facilities were made available to insure prompt and secured transactions.

Infrastructure

To support a strong and growing economy, the government ensured the establishments of proper infrastructures. There are now eight seaports, three international airports and twenty-two domestic airports. A highway network was built throughout the kingdom and a communication system was established at an advanced level.

SUMMARY

Saudi Arabia is the largest country in the Arabian Peninsula in terms of geographic area and population. It is also a fast growing country.

During a relatively short period of time - less than three decades, Saudi Arabia was able to transform itself from an undeveloped nation into a developing nation. Such transformation is no doubt a remarkable achievement.

The development that the kingdom pursued covered all aspects of life. The development of its resources, especially human resources, was apparent should one examine the educational history of the kingdom. The same applies to the industrial, agricultural and communication sectors where development has exceeded world expectation. While all of these developments were made, the kingdom still managed to maintain its Islamic teaching values and traditions.

These developments were positively reflected in the kingdom's economy. The Gross Domestic Product (GDP) grew more than twenty-six times since 1968 and the standard of living has greatly improved.

Saudi Arabia has earned the world's respect and recognition.

SAUDIZATION IN PRACTICE

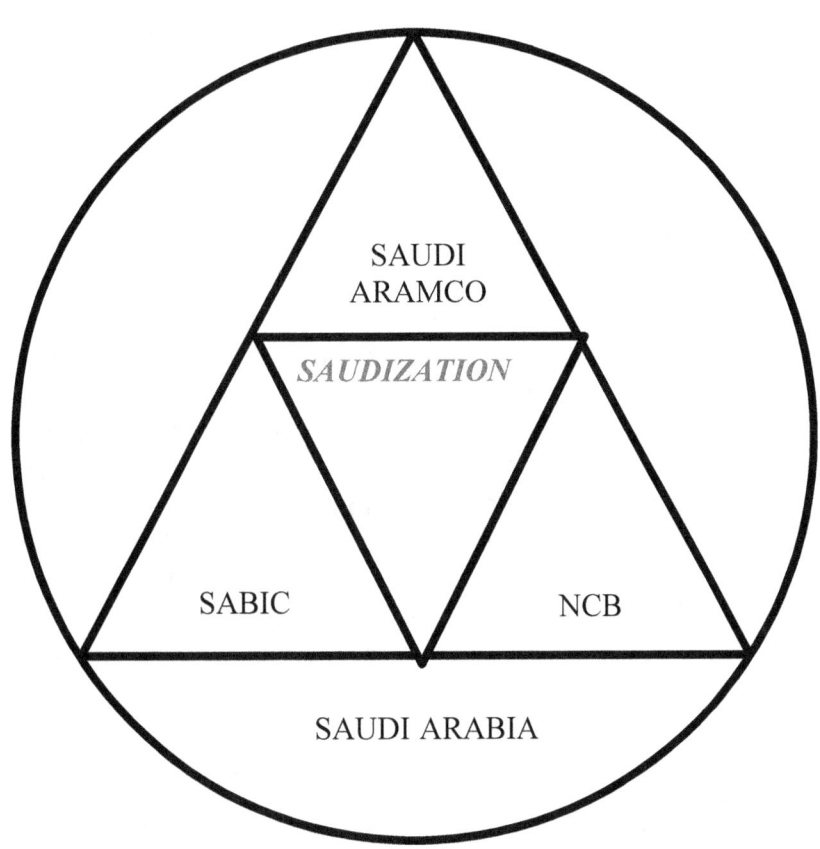

CHAPTER 14

Saudization in Practice

This chapter will highlight the Saudization practices of selected major industries in Kingdom. Their experiences and successes will be the subject of this chapter.

Saudi Aramco

The Saudi Arabian Oil Company (Saudi Aramco) was founded in May 29, 1933 (when the Saudi Arabian Minister and Standard Oil Company of California signed the concession agreement) for the purpose of exploring and producing crude oil, natural gas and its by-products. The head office is located in Dhahran, Eastern province with offices at various places in the world. Currently Saudi Aramco's sustainable crude oil production capacity is 10 million barrels per day costing about US $ 2.5 each barrel. In addition to the gas plants, Saudi Aramco operates five domestic oil refineries and has partnership in two more oil refineries. Also, it has interest in two lube refineries.

Saudi Aramco is adapting a global strategy. It owned 32.5 percent of Motiva Enterprise (Texaco & Shell) in the USA, 35 percent of S-Oil in South Korea, 40 percent of Petron in the Philippine, 50 percent of Motor Oil (Hellas) in Greece and 15 percent in SUMED of Egypt. Presently, negotiations are going on other companies in China, Japan, and Portugal.

Saudi Aramco is also undergoing local expansion with emphasis on Gas production. It is in the process of up grading and expanding its refineries to be able to produce 12 million barrels per day.

Saudi Aramco employs over 55,000 employees of different nationalities and managed by 100 percent nationals. It is a company well known for attracting, retaining, and motivating its employees. It is the pioneer in training and developing nationals who joined the company from various parts of the kingdom. It has a huge training center in Dhahran and training facilities in every major location that the company operates in. These centers are furnished with the latest equipment. In 2002, the Saudization had reached little over 85 percent compared to 41 percent in 1980 (Saudis filling regular jobs- nationals under training and development are not counted). To achieve such a milestone, the company adapted different strategies at different times.

Initially, when skilled and educated nationals were very scarce, the company took upon itself to hire virtually any young Saudis who were interested to work. It provided them with proper education and training in kingdom as well as overseas. As the kingdom's educational system improved and thousands of Saudis became educated, the company was able to recruit Saudis with some education. Those employees who met requirements for higher education would be sent abroad. With time, the company started having access to educated Saudis-not only at high school levels, but at college levels as well.

The company maintains a competitive remuneration package and has a total of seven salary structures (three Western, two Eastern, one for other Arab and one for Saudi Arab). The one for Saudi Arabs consists of 21 salary grades. Below grade 11 is for non-professionals and semi-professionals, while grade 11 to 17 is for professionals and senior professionals. Grade 18 and above are mostly for managers and executives.

The company recruitment is based on a 5 to 10 year manpower plan. The recruiting and training strategies for Saudi Arabs are as follows:

College Graduates (PDP)/(NTG)

There are two categories under college graduates: technical and non-technical majors. The Non-Technical Graduate (NTG) refers to the non-science majors like management, accounting, etc. The Technical Graduate (TC) refers to the science majors such as engineers.

The NTG is usually hired at salary grade 8 and the TC is hired at salary grade 11. All newly hired college graduates undergo a development program. Compared to the NTC, the TC undergoes an intensive program known as *Professional Development Program* (PDP). They remain in the said program for about three years excluding English training if any. During this time, they rotate between different sections or departments performing different jobs as part of their development. Semi-annual performance appraisals are conducted to measure performance and areas that need attention. Such appraisal is associated with a stipend increase. After completion, the employee is considered full-fledged and then called a regular employee.

To illustrate, let us take an engineer for an example and explore his career over a twenty-year period.

Year	Job title	Salary grade
Up to 5 years	Engineer 4- PDP	11
06 -08	Engineer 3	12
09 -12	Engineer 2	13
13 -16	Engineer 1	14
17 +	Engineer, Specialist	15

In addition to filling Engineering positions, many also fill Supervisory and Managerial positions.

High School Graduates (Trainees)

This recruitment covers the science majors, industrial and vocational graduates. These graduates are mainly recruited for operation and maintenance work. With the increasing supply of high school graduates seeking employment, to ensure quality selection, the applicants should have a "very good" rating and undergo a number of tests. The major tests consist of English, Math and General Aptitude Test Battery (GATB). Selected ones sign apprenticeship agreements for two years. During this period, they are called Apprentices (not employees) and administered under the *apprenticeship program*. Upon completion of the apprenticeship program, they are considered employees.

Maintenance program

In maintenance, there are two main types of crafts. Critical crafts like Mechanics, Electricians and Instrument technicians and the metal crafts such as Pipe fitter, Fabricators and Welders. The following illustrates the training scheme for the critical craftsmen.

To produce highly skilled craftsmen, the Apprentices/Trainees go through four phases taking about five years of training. Once completed, they are then placed at salary grade Saudi Arab Regular (SAR) 08. Their further advancement in the field is dependent on their progression in the Individual Development Program (IDP). The training scheme is shown below:

Phase	Type of training	Duration (estimated)
0	English & Math	06 months
1	Common Core program	06 months
2	Specific Discipline courses	12 months
3	On-the-job Training (OJT)- Field	12 months
4	Advanced specialized training + English	12-18 months
—	IDP	—

Operation program

The operation program is different from that of the maintenance. It lasts about three years prior to commencement of OJT covering three phases of training. Once completed, the trainees are placed at SAR 07. The outline of the program is as follows:

Phase	Type of training	Duration (estimated)
0	English + Math	06 months
1	Basic Operator Course	06 months
2.A	Core program	06 months
2.B	Specific training	06 months
3	OJT- Out Side Operator	12 months

Regular Employees

All full job holders are called *regular employees*. They are fully productive and possess the skills and knowledge needed to perform the job of the grade they are holding. However, to keep employees abreast with the latest developments or to prepare one for future promotion, the company provides them with required education and/or training. Sending employees to attend relevant seminars, courses and conferences are prime examples. The company does not hesitate to send highfliers to Europe or the States for higher education or working exposures with other leading oil industries.

To demonstrate how Saudi Aramco provides career development to its employees, one need not go far. Let us take Mr. Ali I. Naimi as one case. Mr. Naimi joined the company as a youth in 1947. He climbed the ladder of professional development through the company's training system holding a number of jobs. In 1983 he was appointed the President of the company. In early 1988, Naimi was named the President and CEO. In 1995 he became the kingdom's Minister of Petroleum and Minerals.

Recruiting and training in Saudi Aramco is a never-ending process. There is always attrition due to employees' retirement, death, disability, resignation or termination. Such actions have a ripple effect as they create an upward movement mainly through promotions. The manpower plan is a very important tool, which is also instrumental in the Saudization process.

To ensure an incoming flow of Saudis, the company takes a proactive role by participating in the annual Career Day at both King Fahad University of Petroleum and Minerals (KFUPM) in Dhahran and King Abdul Aziz University (KAU) in Jeddah. It also has a scholarship program that it offers to selected students and co-op programs with said universities. In addition, the company offers summer jobs for hundreds of students throughout the kingdom. In doing so, it provides working opportunities for the Saudi youth.

SABIC

The Saudi Basic Industries Corporation (SABIC) can be considered a semi-private organization. The Saudi government holds 70 percent of SABIC's ownership while the remaining 30 percent is held by the private sector. It was established in 1976 for the purpose of producing chemicals and petrochemicals, plastic, fertilizers, steel and industrial gases. In 1983 it began its operation. It is based in Riyadh with offices in the USA, Europe and Asia. It has 18 industrial complexes operated by 16 affiliates. SABIC's total sales revenues have surged dramatically from SR 1.9 billion in 1985 to SR 23.59 in 1995. In addition to satisfying the local market, it exports to over 75 countries. In 1995, SABIC produced nearly 23 million tones of petrochemicals.

In an effort to improve efficiency and achieve a competitive edge, SABIC is constantly assessing its business strategies. Expansions, merging some of its projects and consolidating support service functions are momentous. They are adapting the synergy approach where and when possible.

Now, SABIC employed about 16,000 employees. Out of that 12,480 were Saudis making 78 percent of its total manpower. This achievement was accomplished in about twelve years. The question is how?

The following factors went into this accomplishment:

a) The availability of in-kingdom technical and non-technical schools at all levels in addition to the universities. Unlike when Saudi Aramco started when there were minimal schools in the kingdom. Also, the population of Saudis has greatly increased since 1938, making the supply of the work force in better shape than ever before.

b) The labor market was somewhat established by the oil industries. Some workers have left Saudi Aramco and other organizations to join SABIC. This is not to say that SABIC did not have to compete with Saudi Aramco and others like

Petromin, Sececo, banks, etc. There was also competition with the public sector, as the demand of skilled and experienced manpower at that time still exceeded the supply.

c) The foreign partners of SABIC have also contributed to the training and development of the employees. Initially, while the projects were under construction, many Saudis received their training and development abroad, at the partners' facilities. The high school graduates received English, Vocational and On-the-Job Training (OJT), while the college graduates were assigned to different processing units as part of their development program. Upon start-ups of projects at home and as the training was completed, employees returned to their assigned jobs and locations.

d) The early recruitment of Saudis. SABIC selected students at ninth grade and sponsored them for industrial high school education. Once graduated they joined the company as craftsmen trainees. The same applied to college graduates, especially engineers in terms of early recruitment.

e) The determination and zeal of SABIC management at the highest level.

f) The outstanding facilities that Royal Commission for Jubail and Yanbu (RC) provides for the industrial cities where most of SABIC's projects are located.

Furthermore, SABIC also maintains a competitive package for its Saudi employees. The company provides free accommodation, furniture allowance and paid utilities for those living at RC area. There is also a home ownership program for Saudis. The company has five salary structures for different nationalities (Americans, Europeans, other Arabs, Asians and Saudis). The salary grades are from 31 to 48.

Having said that, let us explore SABIC's current (in-kingdom) training and development programs for nationals.

College Graduates (PDE)

All newly college graduates are required to sign a specified period contract when joining the company. They undergo a development program for about two years. During such program they are called Professional Development Employees (PDE). Their performance and development are evaluated every six months with some salary increase for those meeting the requirements. After completion of the program, the PDE signs an employment contract-unspecified period and becomes a full job holder. Again, taking an engineer as an example, the following shows a typical progression:

Year	Job title	Salary grade
0-2	Engineer- PDE	Not applicable
3-5	Engineer	41
6-8	Engineer, advanced	42
9-11	Engineer, senior	43

High School Graduates (Trainees)

For screening purposes, all newly high school as well as technical school graduates undergoes English and aptitude tests. Selected candidates will be placed in a training program. Similar to that of the PDEs, the Trainees are also required to sign a specified period contract-apprenticeship. Once successfully completed, they then sign an employment contract. The program for both maintenance and operation apprentices consist of three stages. After each stage that the Trainee successfully completes, he will receive a salary increase. The program's outlines are as follows:

Maintenance program

Stage	Type of training	Duration(estimated)
1	English	12 months
2	Vocational	09 months
3	OJT- based on tasks	12 months

There are two levels of maintenance workers. One is the craftsman such as Pipe fitters, Carpenters, and Painters. The other one is the technician such as Instruments Analyzers, Electricians, Mechanic, Machinist and Millwright. Once the training program is completed, the craftsmen are placed at salary grade 37 and the technicians are placed at salary grade 38.

Operation program

Stage	**Type of training**	**Duration (estimated)**
1	English	12 months
2	Vocational	03 months
3	OJT	12 months

There are also two levels of operators. Process operators (skilled) and non-process (semi-skilled) operators. The skilled operators are placed at salary grade 37 and the semi- skilled are placed at salary grade 36.

Regular Employees

Employees who joined the company with prior related experience and sign employment contracts (professional or non-processional) are considered regular employees. This also applies to those Trainees and PDEs who have completed their programs and join the productive manpower.

Most of the regular employees go for further development mainly on-the- job, like job rotation and acting assignments for upward movement and promotions. It is they, the regular employees, who are replacing expatriates.

SABIC is also an active participant with the universities and technical schools in kingdom as it is considered to be one of the main employers of Saudis in the region. SABIC also maintains a long-term plan for recruitment and replacement of its manpower. All of their projects are facilitated with training centers and workshops for the purpose of training and educating the Saudi manpower.

National Commercial Bank (NCB)

NCB is classified as a semi-private sector organization. It was founded in 1953 for the purpose of providing all types of banking services by the Bin Mahfouz family. It became a Joint Stock Company on July 1st, 1997. In 1999, the Public Investment Fund (PIF), an arm of the Saudi Government, acquires a 40 percent shareholding in the bank and the Organization for Social Insurance (GOSI) acquires 10 percent. Sheikh Abdullah Salim Bahamdan is currently the Chairman and Managing Director.

NCB is considered to be the oldest Saudi bank and is the largest mutual fund manager in the Kingdom. At year-end 2000, shareholders' fund reached approximately SR 8.0 billion, the largest bank capitalization in the Middle East. Total assets are SR 99.9 billion and its profit exceeded SR 1.5 billion.

NCB has 277 retail-banking branches Kingdom wide and over 600 foreign correspondent banks. NCB adapted the latest technological banking methodology. Its Automatic Teller Machines (ATM) at about 541 machines nationwide. This is in addition to the 1,200 ATMs. NCB also has over 2939 'point of sale' in the Kingdom. The issuance of VISA and Master Cards for in kingdom clients is also one of their strengths.

In 1998 and 1999, Euro money acclaimed NCB "Best Bank in Saudi Arabia". Currently the NCB total number of employees is 4,300. Saudis are 3,300, which represent little over 77 percent of the total manpower. The NCB is aiming for 85 percent by the end of 2004.

NCB maintains a competitive package with an annual review. Currently their package includes three base salaries as housing allowance and three base salaries as a bonus, calculated on a yearly basis but paid monthly. They apply one salary structure, in Saudi Riyals, for all nationalities with a 1-11 grading system.

NCB has three training centers located in three different provinces- Jeddah, Riyadh and Dammam. Each training center works within its own budget. English, Admission and

Psychometric are three tests that all Saudi applicants take before an employment decision is made. Selected ones sign a one-year contract (specified period) during which either party can cease employment. There is no obligation on the part of the employee should he decide to leave during this period. Any employment or training costs are borne by NCB.

High School Graduates

The following shows the progression of the newly hired high school graduates for a *Teller* post:

Year	Salary grade
0-1	not applicable
1+	4

College graduate

The following shows the progression of a college graduate hired as the *Customer Service Representative*:

Year	Salary grade
0-1	not applicable
1+	5

All new hires undergo an induction program for three months and a familiarization program for another three months. During this time, they became familiar with their assignments as well as with the organization climate, culture and mostly its vision. After successfully completing the first year with the bank, the employee signs an open-ended contract and hence becomes a full-fledged employee.

SUMMARY

Saudi Aramco, SABIC and the NCB are the three leading organizations that represent the embodiment of Saudization in kingdom.

Saudi Aramco is the mother of industries in Saudi Arabia. It deals with the oil and Gas industry in the upstream and downstream. Throughout the years it has established its own unique experience in the development and training of Saudis.

SABIC, on the other hand, is the founder of the petrochemical industries in the kingdom. It is considered to be a semi-private organization. It too has its distinguished practices in the Saudization process, techniques and approaches.

NCB is the kingdom's largest bank and the oldest. It represents the private sector of the service industries. NCB also has its own experience in the world of Saudization.

All three organizations were founded at different times and for different lines of business. In that respect, their experiences have been distinctive and diversified. However, they all meet when it comes to Saudization.

CHALLENGES FOR THE FUTURE

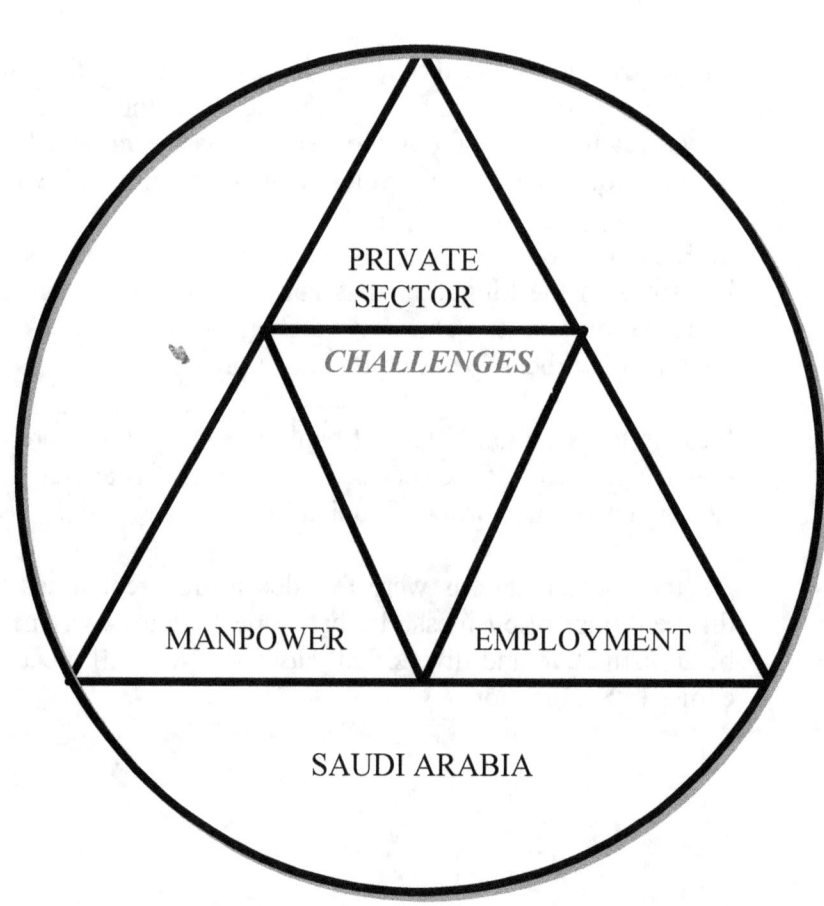

CHAPTER 15

Challenges for the Future

This chapter will explore the challenges ahead. It focuses on the expected future changes for the **private sector, manpower** and **employment**.

Private sector

The kingdom's recent policy is to diversify its income. It no longer wishes to depend on the oil revenue. It is a strategic decision that requires a strategic plan. The plan is to have the private sector play a bigger role in the diversification of income to also include minerals and oil support industries and services. In 2001, the private sector's contribution was about 35 percent of the Kingdom's GDP. This is not sufficient, and a bigger role is demanded. One way of doing so is through privatization.

To facilitate for such role, the government will continue its focus on the two major industrial cities of Jubail and Yanbu. Currently the government is embarking on expanding the facilities especially in the utility areas. By the year 2003, it is anticipated that additional US $ 18 to 20 billion be invested in new industries in the said cities. It is expected that additional major industrial projects be executed jointly between SABIC and the private sector.

Another plan that affects the private sector is the kingdom's intention to become a member of the World Trade Organization (WTO). Members of the WTO will eventually create their own global market, as they will be enjoying a liberalization of trade. The kingdom's membership in the WTO will reflect the industrial export and import of Saudi Arabia. Expected benefits are: 1) paying less import tariff 2) expanding the base of the non-oil industries in the kingdom such as textiles and clothing produced from synthetic fibers.

Having said that, the issues of *privatization, competition, export, environment,* and *technology* are in the private sector priority list.

Privatization

The kingdom's sixth five-year plan (1995-1999) made explicit its intention for the private sector to play a bigger role in future economical growth. Privatization of the nation telecommunication system has been implemented. On the agenda is the Saudi Arabian Airlines (Saudia). The same applies to the electricity companies. Saudi Public Transportation Company, postal services, seaports, education, and health services are also potential organizations for privatization. Increasing the private sector share in SABIC to eventually 75 percent is already in the plan.
It is expected that as the private sector grows the stock market will also grow. This will lead to establishment of joint stock companies in which the private sector will hold interest.

Privatization will most likely take a form of partnership between the government and the private sector whereby the latter will commercially operate said organizations. Different scenarios are being explored. Lease, operate and transfer- LOT is one scenario while build, operate and transfer - BOT is another. There is also the lease, operate and own- LOO and the build, operate and own- BOO scenarios.

Nevertheless, it is expected that the privatization will boost the economy and create jobs for Saudis. Being able to meet these expectations represents a challenge to the private sector.

Competition

The kingdom has adapted a philosophy of a free economy. Import and export are open for business organizations. This invites competition both locally and globally. Therefore, in order for the private sector to survive it has to compete. Competing on the grounds of quality of goods and services, prices, delivery, and value added are the day-to-day solicitudes. For that organizations have adapted the Total Quality Management (TQM) approach in their businesses. ISO 9000 series certifications are in demand and so will be the ISO 14000.

As the kingdom does not work in isolation, events that take place globally also affect the private sector. World Trade Organization (WTO) and other international formations or agreements will indeed affect business at home. It is worth mentioning that WTO replaced the General Agreement on Tariffs and Trade (GATT) that was formed in 1947 with 23 nations. Under the TWO, that number rose to reach 144 member nations in 2002. Their main objectives are to encourage and develop trade between members by obtaining lower tariffs and other rules that favor some countries and disfavor others. It is worth noting that oil and hydrocarbons are not included in the product list of the WTO.

Export

Export generates hard currency for the kingdom. As the private sector matures and is ready to expand its businesses, export becomes the only answer. It has to be. It is the only way to expand the business. Export of Saudi made products is going to be on the increase. To do so, the private sector has to compete globally.

Environment

There are grater concerns for improving the environment by actively saving energy and reducing pollution and waste.

The National Environment Preservation Co. (BeeA'h) has picked up momentum in the kingdom. Their business grew from serving 2 clients and 12 waste streams in 1989 to serving 40 major clients and 441 hazardous or industrial waste streams in 1995.
The intention to produce unleaded fuel to be used in Saudi Arabia is another indication of the government's concern for the environment.

It is expected that new legislation will be imposed in the area of a) saving water and energy b) reducing pollution and c) reducing waste. In doing so, new industries will most likely be formed for the purpose of material recycling and remanufacturing.

Technology

Technology is ever changing more now than ever before. As indicated in Chapter 4, the kingdom and its private sector are adapting the latest technology.

The introduction of facsimile, electronic mail (E mail), cellular phones and now the Internet are prime examples of what technology can do to improve the business and communication. This is in addition to the advanced control systems and programs that many organizations are using in the operation processes. The introduction of SAP and Oracle technology are also prime example. Technology will play a major roll for those wishing to gain a competitive advantage. Technology will provide them with the tool to increasing productivity, reliability and operating flexibility.

The technology will continue to change especially in the way of creating, storing, sorting, using, and sharing information and data. Those organizations that are not catching up will most likely vanish.

Future, emphases will not only be on consuming technology but on producing it as well. Therefore, it is expected that the private sector actively participates in the establishment of research and development (R&D) centers. R&D is the key to future success and prosperity.

The Kingdom of Saudi Arabia has already taken serious steps in adapting today's technology. Applying the principal of "e-government" and introducing "e-commerce" are on the horizon. Such development can only benefit the business of tomorrow.

Manpower

As indicated in Chapter 13 of this book, the Saudi manpower is growing. Today, with a total population of only 23 million, unemployment rate exceeds 15 percent. It is estimated that by the year 2020, the population will increase to more than 29 million. Private sector is already faced with the challenge of Saudization as is. Can you imagine what would it be in 2020?

If privatization is to take place, one can expect a release of surplus manpower (redundancy) that is currently absorbed by the public sector. This can only add to the challenges ahead.

Employment

A report by the Civil Services Bureau covering the period 1994-95 indicated that the total number of employees working with the government is 609,000. Of these 21 percent are expatriates. The majority is working in the education and health areas. This number has been reduced by now to less than 10 percent, yet the number of expatriates in the kingdom is high as they still make 53 percent of the total work force. Since the majority of the expatriates are working in the private sector, it is naturally that Saudization at the private sector be activated.

This situation has led the Council of Ministers to activate Article 50 of the Labor and workmen Law that dictates an annual increase of 5 percent of Saudization in the private sector.

It is anticipated that further restrictions be imposed for employing expatriates. Employment will be confined to Saudis with the exception of a few jobs or disciplines. Employing Saudis requires that they be competitive and skilled. It also demands high working values and ethics. Value for money attitude will be widely adapted by business organizations. Jobs that most Saudis do not hold today will be held by them tomorrow. The same applies to the work locations and the working hours. Employment at the public sector, which many

Saudis prefer mainly due to job security and working hours, will be limited.

To create skilled Saudis, the private sector will be involved in their training and education. This involvement will not be limited to that of employers only, but also in the establishment of businesses for the purpose of producing and recruiting an employable work force. It is predicted that major companies in the region such as Saudi Aramco will participate in the mass training of nationals.

The current educational system will also be modified to coincide with the private sector's requirements and with the latest technology. The General Organization for Social Insurance Law (GOSI) has been already amended to include early retirement program. The Labor and Workmen Law is next on the amendment agenda where emphasize on performance will be placed. Recruitment of expatriates, visa issuance and residence permit renewals will also be tightened. Improving expatriates living and working conditions and benefits such as health and dental care are to be expected. Those organizations that do not meet the Saudization quota will most probably be disqualified from government loans, facilities, and tenders' participation. The local media will also be activated to serve these goals. All of which will eventually make hiring expatriates a less attractive exercise.

Imposing minimum wages is something one can foresee happening in the near future. Similarly, private sector should not expect the government to further subsidize the cost of training the nationals.

Female search for employment at the private sector is also anticipated to pick up a momentum as there will be more female available for work. It is noted that currently the female workers represent only 7 percent of the total workforce in the Kingdom.

Let there be no mistake. There are no real alternatives but to meet the challenges ahead. To effectively achieve an indigenous manpower is the responsibility of all concerned and that something we should never forget.

I do hope that businessmen and stakeholders at the private sector be more serious in the Saudization issue and take proactive measures. Also, they should take advantage of the somewhat relaxant rules and regulations currently applied for Saudization and start their plans accordingly. Before a day comes when they would have lost the opportunity to serve their organization better. Then, it will be late, and they will be ill prepared. And that day will definitely come.

SUMMARY

Changes bring challenges especially if the change is rapid and fundamental.

The private sector is invited to play a much bigger role than before. The private sector is invited to increase its contribution to the GDP by means of export and expansions. The private sector is invited to help diversify the national income where oil does not represent the bulk of it. The private sector is also invited to gradually take over some of the public sector's organizations by means of privatization. To become the government's business partner in commercially running certain sectors is the challenge awaiting the private sector.

The private sector also needs to play a bigger role in conserving energy and reducing waste and pollution. Preserving the environment, we live in and the air we breathe will be a future top priority.

The world is becoming smaller as technology grows and globalization intrudes itself. The private sector is requested to keep pace with the latest trends in the world of technology in order to survive.

Other challenges are the growing Saudi manpower and their employment in the private sector. How can the Saudis meet the expectations of the private sector in terms of cost, skills, and productivity, yet be able to compete locally and globally?

These challenges and more are in store for the private sector in the years ahead.

Bibliography

Selected Books

Adam, J. H. Longman. Dictionary of Business English. Beirut: York Press, 1989.

Champy, James. Reengineering Management: The Mandate for New Leadership. New York: Harper Business, 1995.

ITN Factbook. London: Michael O'Mara Books Limited, 1990.

The Noble Qur'an. Translated by Dr. Muhammad Taqi-ud-Din Al-Hilali, Ph.D. And Dr. Muhammad Muhsin Khan.

Perry, John A. Contemporary Society. San Francisco: Canfield Press, 2nd. Ed., 1975

Saudi Aramco And Its World: Arabia And The Middle East. Houston: Aramco Services Company, 1995

Tracey, William R. The Human Resources Glossary: A Complete Desk Reference For HR Professionals. New York: AMACOM, 1991.

Yergin, Daniel. The Prize. New York: Simon & Schuster, 1991.

Selected Articles and Reports

Saudi American Bank, Report on" the Saudi Economy in 2002"

MEED Special Report, Saudi Arabia (April 1996).

MEIRC Monthly Report (July 1995).

The National Commercial Bank Annual Report (1995).

National Day Supplement. Arab News, Vol XXI No. 300, September 23, 1996.

"Our future challenges." Arab News, Vol XXI No. 289, September 13, 1996.

"The present and past of industrial development." Arab News, Vol XXI No. 306, September 29, 1996.

"Rapid population growth a big challenge." Arab News, March 29, 2000.

SABIC Annual Report (1995).
"SABIC is poised for steady growth." Arab News, Vol XXI No. 306, September 29, 1996.
Saudi Aramco Brochure- Yanbu online for the future (January 1993).
"UAE unemployment 'far worse than West'." Middle East Expatriate, Vol XIII No. 4 (May 1, 1996)
"Yanbu growing fast, growing prosperous." Saudi Gazette, September 23, 1996.

Selected Web Sites

http://www.alahli.com
http://www.arabia.com
http://www.saudiaramco.com
http://www.sabic.com

Arabic Bibliography

المراجع باللغة العربية:
أولا الكتب:

1- حامد عبد السلام زهران. علم النفس الإجتماعي (القاهرة: عالم الكتب، الطبعة الخامسة، 1984م).

2- ---------- التوجيه والإرشاد النفسي (القاهرة: عالم الكتب، الطبعة الثانية، 1980م)

3- سليم كامل درويش. الإقتصاد الصناعي: تشكيله-فعاليته وموقع المملكة العربية السعودية من تقنياته (جدة: تهامة، 1985).

4- سعيد يس عامر وعلي محمد عبد الوهاب. الفكر المعاصر في التنظيم الإداري (القاهرة: مركز وايد سيرفس للإستشارات و التطوير الإداري، 1994م).

5- عاصم بن طاهر عرب. إقتصاديات العمل- نظرية عامة (الرياض: جامعة الملك سعود 1994م).

6- عبد الرحمن صادق الشريف. جغرافية المملكة العربية السعودية (الرياض: دار المريخ للنشر، الطبعة الرابعة 1994م).

7- عبدالله المحمد الخريجي ومحمد الجوهري. التنمية الإجتماعية (جدة: ملتزم التوزيع، 1986م).

8- كامل بكري. التنمية الإقتصادية (بيروت: دار النهضة العربية للطباعة والنشر، 1986).

9- محمد حامد عبدالله. إقتصاديات الموارد (الرياض: جامعة الملك سعود، 1991م).

10- محمد علي محمد. الشباب العربي والتغير الإجتماعي (الإسكندرية: دار المعرفة الجامعية 1987م).

11- مصطفى نجيب شاويش. إدارة الأفراد (عمان: دار الشروق للنشر والتوزيع، 1990م).

ثانيا الجرائد والمجلات:

1- الرياض: "دراسة: الإقتصاد السعودي الأكثر تزايدا في التنوع والتقدم." العدد 10318، 23 سبتمبر 1996م.

2- الشرق الأوسط: "أرامكو تسعى إلى رفع طاقاتها التكريرية الى 4 ملايين برميل يوميا". العدد 6525، 9 أكتوبر 1996م.

3- الشرق الأوسط: "أبا الخيل: العلاقات الإقتصادية السعودية – الأمريكية من بداية للتفاهم الى تبادل للمصالح". العدد 6523، 7 أكتوبر 1996م.

4- الشرق الأوسط: "إستكمال المرحلة الأولى لبرنامج تخصيص الموانىء.." العدد 7290، 13 نوفمبر 1998م.

5- الشرق الأوسط:"تخصيص خدمات البريد السعودية.." العدد 7093، 30 إبريل 1998م.
6- الشرق الأوسط:"100 مليار دولار تحويلات العمالة الأسيوية من دول الخليج.." العدد 8171، 12 إبريل 2001م.
7- الشرق الأوسط: "الإقتصاد السعودي ينتظر إقرار أنظمة التجارة الإلكترونية" العدد8182، 23 إبريل 2001م.
8- الشرق الأوسط: "مؤتمر الحكومة الإلكترونية يبدأ فعالياته في الرياض.." العدد 8540، 16 إبريل 2002م.
9- الشرق الأوسط: "إرتفاع تحويلات العمالة الأجنبية .." العدد 8564 ، 10 مايو 2002م.
10- الإقتصادية: "الضغط على المرافق العامة أبرز محازير تشغيل الأجانب". العدد 1152، 5 أكتوبر 1996م.
11- الإقتصادية: "الإستقرار السياسي يبلور المنظور السعودي للتنمية." العدد 1140، 23 سبتمبر 1996م.
12- الإقتصادية: "الملك فهد في حديث شامل عشية ذكرى اليوم الوطني السعودي." العدد 1140 ، 23 سبتمبر 1996م.
13- الإقتصادية: " الفنيون الأكثر طلبا للعمل في القطاع الخاص." العدد 1150، 3 أكتوبر 1996م.
14- الإقتصادية: " من يسعود من؟" العدد 1164، 71 أكتوبر 1996م.
15- الإقتصادية: " طفرة مقبلة في الجبيل وينبع" العدد 1177، 30 أكتوبر 1996م.
16- الإقتصادية: " وزير البترول السعودي يعلن تأسيس شركة جديدة" العدد 1197، 19 نوفمبر 1996م.
17- الإقتصادية: "ندرة الوظائف ليست عائقا أمام السعوديات" العدد 1891، 13 نوفمبر 1998م.
18- الإقتصادية: "15% نسبة البطالة بين السعوديين" العدد 3125، 1 مايو 2002م.
19- الأسواق: العدد 17 (السنة الثانية) ، إبريل 1996م.
20- عالم المال والأعمال: "الإقتصاد" (السنة الثانية) ، يناير 1997م.
21- قافلة الزيت: "السعودة من أهم أهداف الشركة" ، 28 شعبان 1417هـ

Appendixes

Appendix I is a flowchart that summarizes the process involved in the replacement of expatriates:

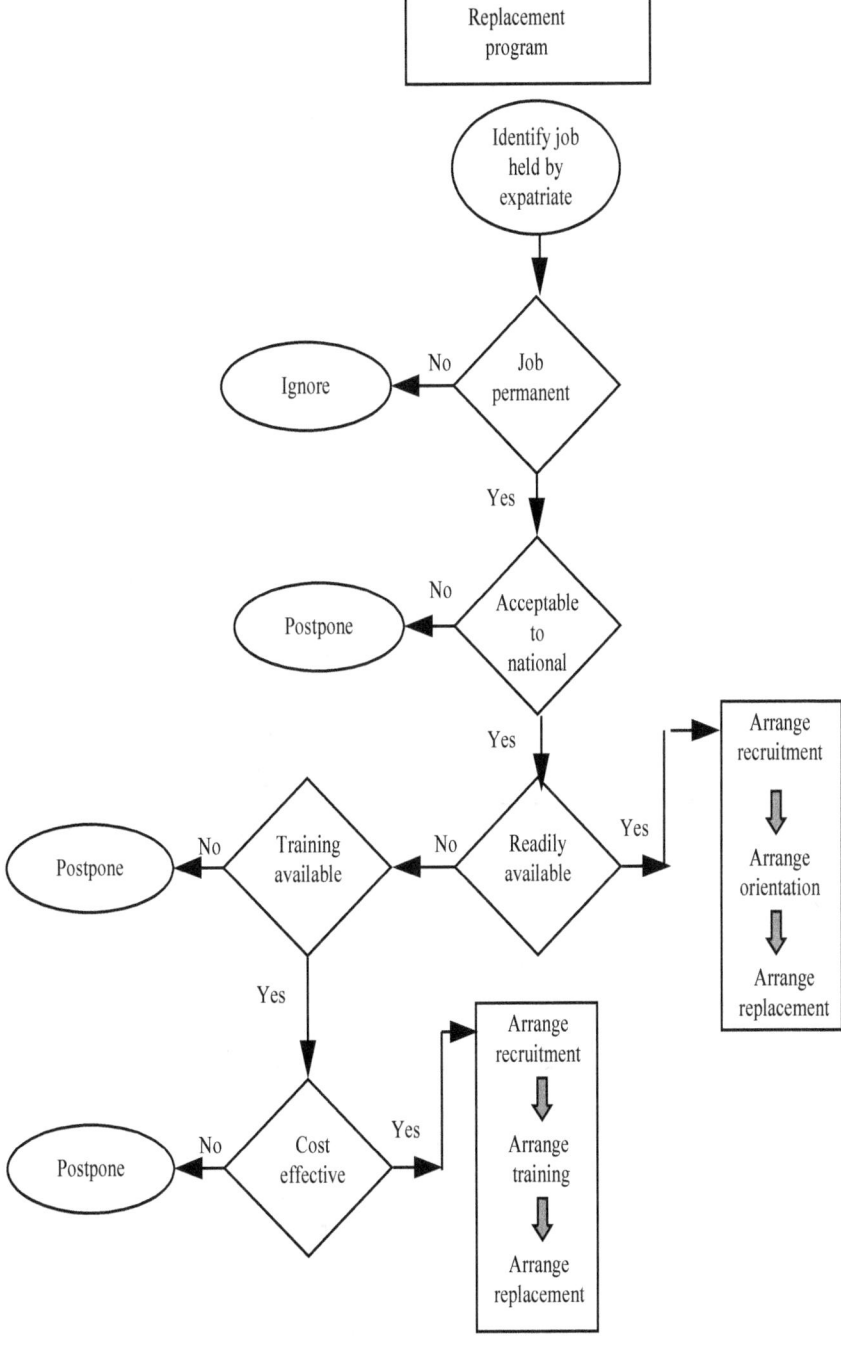

Appendix II is a flowchart that summarizes the process involved in jobs selection of local applicants:

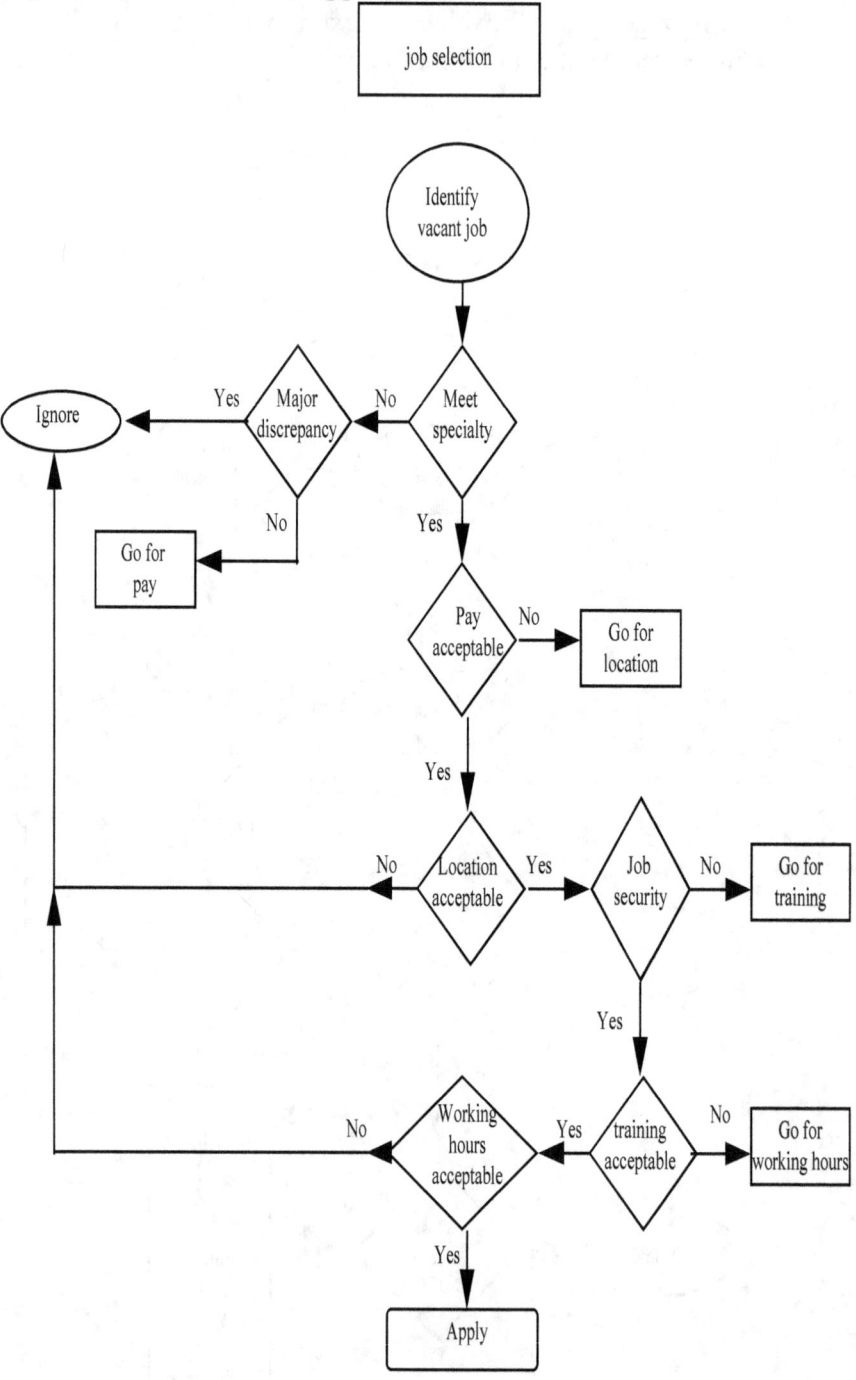

Index

Agriculture, 103
Banks, 104
Competition, 121
Economy, 101
Education, 100
Employment, 25, 124
    objectives, 26
    activities, 26
    resources, 28
Environment, 122
Environmental factors, 37
    family as, 37
    mosques as, 38
    schools as, 39
Establish the Plan 82
    business direction, 82
    organization structure, 83
    manpower plan, 85
    work rules, 88
Evaluate the Business, 76
    business as is today, 77
    business at maximum indigenous work force, 78
    business in light of tomorrow, 77
Expatriates, 51
    who are they? 51
    why are they here and what do they do? 52
    what are their working and living conditions? 52
    what are the implications? 53
Execute the Plan, 90
    by hiring the team leader, 90
    by setting recruiting strategy, 91
    by replacement strategy, 93
    by succession plan, 94
Export, 122

Influencing factors, 30
    variables as, 32
    environment as, 37
    values as, 42
Investment, 66
    cost of, 66
    gain from, 72
    risk of, 71
Job analysis, 84
Job classification schedule, 85
Job category, 27
    activities of, 26
    objectives of, 19
    resources of, 21
Manpower, 18
    activities of, 20
    objectives of, 19
    resources of, 21
NCB, 116-118
Organization structure, 84
Private sector, 11, 116
    activities of, 13
    objectives of, 12
    resources of, 14
Privatization, 121
Population, 99
SABIC, 112-115
    see also private sector
Saudi Arabia, 97
    development in focus of, 99
    Saudization in practice of, 107
    challenges in the future of, 120

SAUDI ARAMCO, 107-111
Security and social risks, 54
Succession plan, 94
Team leader, 90
Technology, 123
Technology transfer and beyond, 54
Unemployment, 56
Value factors, 42
    for individuals, 45
    for organizations, 43
    for work, 46
Variable factors, 32
    economy as, 33
    population as, 32
    technology & legislation as, 34
Work rules, 88

www.ingramcontent.com/pod-product-compliance
Lightning Source LLC
Chambersburg PA
CBHW051317220526
45468CB00004B/1382